Sport Eye, An Encyclopedia Of Sports

Every record herein con-
tained is authentic and accu-
rate, having been obtained
from sources which are affili-
ated very closely with that
very sport.

If the reader obtains as
much enjoyment and pleasure
from the perusal of SPORT-CYC
as the author had in compil-
ing same, the purpose of this
little volume will not have
gone amiss.

THE AUTHOR

INDEX

BASEBALL

World's Records of Baseball Hitting

Miscellaneous Baseball Records

11

16

BASEBALL

WORLD'S PITCHING RECORDS

Most Games Pitched During a Season
75—William White, Cincinnati, N. L., 1879.

Most Games Won During a Season
60—Charles Radbourne, Providence, N. L., 1884.

Most Games Lost During a Season
29—Vic Willis, Boston, N. L., 1905.
26—John Townsend, Washington, A. L., 1904.
26—Bob Groom, Washington, A. L., 1909.

Highest Percentage of Games Won
.899—Al G. Spalding, Boston, N. A., 1875.
.872—Joe Wood, Boston, A. L., 1912.
.842—Tom Hughes, Boston, N. L., 1916.

Most Times at Bat by Opponents
1690—Ed. Walsh, Chicago, A. L., 1908.
1531—Grover C. Alexander, Philadelphia, N. L., 1917.

Most Innings Pitched
464—Ed. Walsh, Chicago, A. L., 1908.
389—G. C. Alexander, Philadelphia, N. L., 1916.

Most Hits by Opponents
360—Jack Coombs, Athletics, A. L., 1911.
357—G. C. Alexander, Philadelphia, N. L., 1914.

Hit Most Batsmen
41—Joe McGinnity, New York, A. L., 1900.
26—Jack Warhop, New York, A. L., 1909.

Most Bases on Balls—Season

276—Amos Rusie, New York, N. L., 1890.

168—Elmer Myers, Athletics, A. L., 1916.

Most Bases on Balls—Game

20—Davidson, Baltimore, Aug. 4, 1914.

20—Harper, Minneapolis, July 5, 1915.

17—William George, New York, N. L., May 30, 1887.

'16—Ben Haas, Athletics, A. L., June 23, 1915.

Strike Out Records—Game

20—Dailey, Chicago, N. L., vs. Boston, 1884.

19—Sweeney, Providence, N. L., vs. Boston, 1883.

16—Glade, St. Louis, A. L., vs. Washington, 1904.

16—Waddell, St. Louis, A. L., vs. Athletics, 1908.

17—Ramsey, Louisville, A. A. vs. Cleveland, 1887.

(Ramsey pitched when 4 strike rule was in vogue. His record is equal to about 22 strike-outs under present rule.)

Strike Out Records—Season

505—Kilroy, Baltimore, 1886.

494—Ramsey, Louisville, 1886.

469—Dailey, Chicago Unions, 1884.

459—Shaw, Washington, 1884.

402—Buffington, Providence, 1884.

367—Van Greeg, Portland, 1910.

352—Sweeney, Providence, 1884.

344—Keefe, New York, N. L., 1888.
343—Waddell, Athletics, 1904.
342—Rusie, New York, N. L., 1891.
334—Henderson, Baltimore, 1884.
325—Clarkson, Chicago, 1886.
313—Johnson, Washington, A. L., 1908.
313—Morris, Louisville. 1888.

Most Consecutive Shut Out Innings
78—A. Faulkner, Wilmington, Del., 1903.
59—Wilhelm, Birmingham, S. L., 1911.
56—Walter Johnson, Washington, A. L., 1913.
41—Chesbro, Pittsburgh, N. L., 1902.
41—Alexander, Philadelphia, N. L., 1911.

Most Consecutive Games Won—Season
21—Baxter Sparks, Yazoo City, Delta League, 1904.
19—Tim Keefe. New York, N. L., 1888.
19—R. W. Marquard, New York, N. L., 1912.
16—Walter Johnson, Washington, A. L., 1912.
16—Jos. Wood, Boston, A. L., 1912.

Most No-Hit Games Pitched—Season
4—Pitcher Juskus, Lancaster, 1908.
3—Larry Corcoran, Chicago, N. L., 1880-82-84.

No Man Reaches First Base
G. W. Bradley, St. Louis, N. L., July 15, 1876.
John Richmond, Worcester, N. L., June 12, 1880.
J. M. Ward, Providence, N. L., June 17, 1880.

D. T. Young, Boston, A. L., May 5, 1904.

Addie Joss, Cleveland, A. L., Oct. 2, 1908.

Most Chances Accepted Per Season

262—Ed. Walsh, Chicago, A. L., 1907..

Game

13—Ed. Walsh, Chicago, A. L., 1907.

Most Assists Per Season

227—Ed. Walsh, Chicago, A. L., 1907.

203—McMahon, Baltimore, A. A., 1890.

Most Bases on Balls Received—Season

Club

681—Detroit, A. L., 1915.

655—St. Louis, N. L., 1910.

Player

148—Babe Ruth, New York, A. L., 1920.

147—James Sheckard, Chicago, N. L., 1911.

Most Bases on Balls Received—Game

Club

18—Detroit, A. L., 1916.

16—Cincinnati, N. L., 1910.

Player

11—Consecutive walks. Outfielder Nick De Maggio, Beaumont team, Texas League, Sept. 2, 4 and 5, 1910. Sept. 2, last three times he walked. Sept. 3, rain. Sept. 4, drew five passes in 5 times at bat. On Sept. 5, three.

6—Walter Wilmot, Chicago, N. L., Aug. 22, 1891.

6—Harry Hulen, Minneapolis, A. A., Aug. 1, 1894.

6—J. Woodsen, Charlotte, Carolina Assn., May 19, 1911.

Struck Out Most Times in One Season

Club

863—St. Louis, A. L., 1914.

706—Brooklyn, N. L., 1910.

Player

120—Williams, St. Louis, A. L., 1914.

89—C. Cravath, Phila., N. L., 1916.

Most Put Outs by Pitcher—Season

49—Nick Altrock, Chicago, A. L., 1904.

Most Put Outs by Pitcher—Game

5—Lou Wiltse, Baltimore, A. L., 1902.

5—Joe Wood, Boston, A. L., 1912.

Most Assists by Pitcher—Game

11—Jueitt Meekin, Washington, N. L., 1893.

11—Harry Gardner, Oakland, P. C. L., July 31, 1921.

11—Ed. Walsh, Chicago, A. L., 1907.

11—Geo. McConnell, New York, A. L., 1912.

11—Mel Wolfgang, Chicago, A. L., 1914.

Most Errors by Pitcher—Season

15—Jack Chesbro, New York, A. L., 1904.

15—Rube Waddell, Athletics, A. L., 1905.

15—Ed. Walsh, Chicago, A. L., 1912.

Most Errors by Pitcher Per Game

11—James Hagen, Philadelphia, N. L., 1883.

Most Wild Pitches—Season

30—Leon Ames, New York, N. L., 1905.

21—Walter Johnson, Washington, A. L., 1910.

Most Wild Pitches Per Game

5—Jas. Hagen, Philadelphia, N. L., Aug. 21, 1883.

5—Larry Cheney. Brooklyn, N. L., July 9, 1918.

4—Walter Johnson, Washington, A. L., June 19, 1909.

Most Shut-Out Games Per Season
Player
16—G. C. Alexander, Phila., N. L., 1917.

13—Jack Coombs, Athletics, A. L., 1910.

Club
89—Portland, Pacific Coast League. 1910.

82—Portland, Pacific Coast League, 1913.

54—Lincoln, W. L., 1912.

52—Pittsburgh, N. L., 1903.

Three Year Consecutive Record
(30 or More Wins)

Mathewson—1903, 30; 1904, 33; 1905, 31. New York, N. L.

Alexander—1915, 31; 1916, 33; 1917, 30. Philadelphia, N. L.

YOUNG'S WONDERFUL RECORD

Twenty-two Years In Game

With National League 12 Years

Games	W.	L.	PCT.
464	291	173	.648

American League 10 Years

Games	W.	L.	PCT.
355	217	138	.611

Recapitulation

	Years	W.	L.	PCT.
National League.....	12	291	173	.648
American League.....	10	217	138	.611
Totals	22	508	311	.620

Three Year Record

1901, 31 wins; 1902, 32 wins; 1903, 28 wins.

In his career Young pitched three no-hit games. In the second game, not a man reached first.

RECORD PITCHING FEATS

Sept. 8, 1910—Tucker of Bessemer team, Birmingham held his opponents to two "no-hit" games in one afternoon.

1908—Pitcher Durham when pitching for Indianapolis (American Association) pitched five double-headers in a season and won all ten games.

1884—Charles Radbourne of Providence, pitched 80 full games. 72 were for the championship, 5 exhibitions, and 3 world series contests.

1908—Walter Johnson of Washington (A. L.) shut out the Yankees in three consecutive games on three consecutive playing days. (Sept. 4-5-7, 6th being on a Sunday.)

Addie Joss has two "no-hit" games to his credit.

PITCHING RECORDS
Chas. ("Babe") Adams

Born, Tipton, Ind., May 18, 1883.

In 1920, Adams led the National League in shut-out games (8), second to Alexander in point of earned runs scored. In the 35 full games he pitched, he issued but 18 bases on balls, hit one batsman, pitched 263 innings, faced 1,035 batsmen. So splendid in his "control" he issued one pass for each 15 innings he pitched. The most remarkable pitching feat ever credited to any pitcher was in 1914, when he pitched 21 innings against the New York Giants, failed to either issue a base on balls, hit a batter, or make a wild pitch.

ADAMS' PITCHING RECORD

Year	W	L	H	BB	S.O.	H.B.	W.P.	PCT.
1909	12	3	150	23	65	2	2	.800
1910	18	9	217	60	101	6	1	.667
1911	22	12	253	42	133	8	3	.647
1912	11	8	169	35	63	3	0	.579
1913	10	4	271	49	144	0	5	.714
1914	13	16	253	39	91	7	2	.448
1915	14	14	229	34	62	2	2	.500
1916	2	9	90	12	21	3	1	.182
1917	(With Hutchinson, Kan., Western League)							
1918	1	1	16	4	6	0	0	.500
1919	17	10	213	23	92	3	2	.630
1920	17	13	240	18	84	1	5	.567
1921	15	6	—	—	—	—	—	.737
	152	105	2091	339	862	35	23	.659

ADAMS' FIELDING RECORDS

Year	G	P.O.	A	E	T.C.	PCT
1909	25	1	35	3	37	.919
1910	34	7	44	5	56	.911
1911	40	3	42	1	46	.978
1912	28	2	36	0	38	1.000
1913	43	10	74	1	85	.988
1914	40	13	62	0	75	1.000
1915	40	3	67	0	70	1.000
1916	16	2	20	0	22	1.000
1917	(Not in Majors)					
1918	3	0	39	0	5	1.000
1919	34	4	55	0	59	1.000
1920	35	3	66	2	71	.972
12	338	48	508	12	564	.979

WORLD'S RECORDS OF FIRST BASEMEN

Highest Fielding Average

.999—J. McInnis, Boston, A. L., 1921.
.997—Walter L. Holke, Boston, N. L., 1921.

Most Chances Per Season

1986—Jiggs Donohue, Chicago, A. L., 1907.

Most Put-Outs Per Season

1846—Jiggs Donohue, Chicago, A. L., 1907.

Most Assists Per Season

152—Fred Tenney, Boston, N. L., 1905.

Most Errors Per Season

86—William Joyce, New York, N. L., 1898.

Most Put-outs Per Game

22—Charles Houtz, St. Louis, N. Association, June 3, 1875.

22—W. T. O'Brien, Washington, N. L., September 22, 1888.

22—Jake Beckley, Cincinnati, N. L., September 27, 1898.

22—Tom Jones, St. Louis, A. L., May 11, 1906.

22—Hal Chase, New York, A. L., Sept. 21, 1906.

22—Jake Daubert, Brooklyn, N. L., May 6, 1910.

22—Hal Chase, New York, A. L., June 23, 1911.

22—Ed. Konetchy, Pittsburg, N. L., Sept. 4, 1914.

22—John McInnis, Boston, A. L., July 19, 1918.

Most Assists Per Game

7—W. E. Bransfield, Pittsburg, N. L., May 3, 1904.

7—George Stovall, St. Louis, N. L., Aug. 7, 1912.

7—Fred Luderus, Philadelphia, N. L., Aug. 22, 1919.

Most Errors Per Game

5—Roger Connor, Troy, N. L., May 27, 1882.

4—Hal Chase, New York, A. L., July 23, 1913.

No Put-Outs at First Base

Mutuals, N. Y. vs. Alpine Club, July 21, 1861.

Guy Hecker, Louisville, A. A., Oct. 9, 1887.

McCauley, Wash. A. A. vs. Columbus, Aug. 6, 1891.

J. Donohue, Chicago, A. L. vs. New York A. L., May 23, 1906.

Jack Ernst, Canton vs. Dayton, June 28, 1906.

Bill Emerson, Monson, Mass. vs. Stafford, Conn., Aug. 12, 1906.

Artie Hofman, Chicago, N. L., vs. Pittsburg, June 24, 1910.

Connors, Terre Haute vs. South Bend, July 10, 1910.

McGamwell, Haverhill vs. Worcester, May 20, 1911.

Schineel, Hartford vs. Bridgeport, July 18, 1911.

Pressley, Roanoke vs. Norfolk, July 2, 1913.

Kelliher, Worcester vs. Fitchburg, June 14, 1915.

Brief, Salt Lake vs. Vernon, Sept. 8, 1915.

1—Donohue, one assist; Hofman, one error.

WORLD'S RECORDS OF SECOND BASEMEN

Highest Fielding Average Per Season
991—Larry Lajoie, Cleveland, A. L., 1905.

Most Chances Per Season
988—Larry Lajoie, Cleveland, A. L., 1908.
934—William Sweeney, Boston, N. L., 1912.

Most Chances Per Game
19—Miller Huggins, St. Paul, A. A., Sept. 17, 1902.

18—Fred Dunlap, Cleveland, N. L., July 24, 1882.

16—Larry Lajoie, Athletics, A. L., Sept. 24, 1901.

16—Del Pratt, New York, A. L., April 26, 1920.

Most Put-outs Per Season
477—James Williams, New York, A. L., 1903.
459—William Sweeney, Boston, N. L., 1912.

Most Put-outs Per Game
12—George Hawks, Troy, N. L., July 30, 1879.
10—Hobe Ferris, Boston, A. L., May 13, 1901.

Most Assists Per Season
538—Larry Lajoie, Cleveland, A. L., 1908.
536—Louis Bierbauer, Pittsburg, N. L., 1892.

Most Assists Per Game

12—Fred Dunlap, Cleveland, N. L., July 24, 1882.

11—Joe Gedeon, St. Louis, A. L., May 22, 1918.

11—Del Pratt, New York, A. L., April 26, 1920.

Most Errors Per Season

88—Charles Smith, Cincinnati, N. L., 1880.

88—Charles Ferguson, Philadelphia, N. L., 1883.

61—William Gilbert, Milwaukee, A. L., 1901.

61—William (Kid) Gleason, Detroit, A. L., 1901.

Most Errors Per Game

8—Andy Leonard, Boston, N. L., June 14, 1876.

5—Charles Hickman, Washington, A. L., Sept. 29, 1905.

WORLD'S RECORDS OF THIRD BASEMEN

Highest Fielding Average Per Season

986—Oscar Vitt, Detroit, A. L., 1920.

Most Chances Per Season

658—Charles Smith, Newcastle, Ohio, State League, 1898.

601—James Collins, Boston, N. L., 1899.

593—Oscar Vitt, Detroit, A. L., 1916.

Most Chances Per Game

14—Jiggs Parrott, Chicago, N. L., June 5, 1893.

13—Joe Battin, Pittsburg, A. A., April 20, 1883.

12—Sam Strang, Chicago, A. L., July 4, 1902.

Most Put-outs Per Season

252—Jimmy Collins, Boston, N. L., 1899.

239—William Coughlin, Kansas City, A. L., 1900.

Most Put-outs Per Game

8—Arthur Devlin, New York, N. L., May 23, 1908.

8—Milton Stock, Philadelphia, N. L., May 24, 1917.

8—Douglas Baird, St. Louis, N. L., June 17, 1918.

7—Sam Strang, Chicago, A. L., July 4, 1902.

Most Assists Per Season

402—Jay Andrews, Buffalo, A. L., 1900.

384—William Shindle, Baltimore, N. L., 1892.

Most Assists Per Game

11—Jerry Denny, New York, N. L., May 29, 1890.

9—George, "Buck" Weaver, Chicago, A. L., June 3, 1920.

Most Errors Per Season

91—Charles Hickman, New York, N. L., 1900.

73—William Nance, Minneapolis, A. L., 1900.

Most Errors Per Game

6—Joe Mulvey, Philadelphia, N. L., July 30, 1884.

WORLD'S RECORDS OF SHORT-STOPS

Highest Average Per Season
976—Everett Scott, Boston, A. L., 1918.

Most Chances Per Season
981—Walter Maranville, Boston, N. L., 1914.
969—Owen Bush, Detroit, A. L., 1914.

Most Chances Per Game
20—Dave Forse, Buffalo, N. L., Sept. 15, 1881.
19—Dan Richardson, Washington, N. L., June 20, 1892.
19—Fred Parent, Boston, A. L., July 8, 1902.
17—Rhody Wallace, St. Louis, A. L., June 10, 1902.

Most Put-outs Per Season
433—Bob Allen, Philadelphia, N. L., 1892.
425—Owen Bush, Detroit, A. L., 1914.

Most Put-outs Per Game
11—William Fuller, New York, N. L., Aug. 20, 1895.
10—Larry Lajoie, Philadelphia, A. L., Sept. 24, 1901.

Most Assists Per Season
598—Dave Bancroft, New York, N. L., 1920.
570—Topsy Turner, Cleveland, A. L., 1906.

Most Assists Per Game
14—Tommy Corcoran, Cincinnati, N. L., Aug. 7, 1903.

12—Norman Elberfeld, Detroit, A. L., Sept. 2, 1901.

Most Errors Per Season
115—Billy Shindle, Philadelphia, N. L., 1890.
106—Jos. Sullivan, Washington, N. L., 1883.
95—Jake Gochnaur, Cleveland, A. L., 1903.

Most Errors Per Game
7—John Hallinan, Mutuals, N. Y., July 29, 1876.
7—John Smith, Buffalo, A. L., May 29, 1900.

WORLD'S RECORDS OF OUT-FIELDERS

Highest Fielding Average Per Season
992—Hans Wagner, Pittsburg, N. L., 1902.
992—Frank Schulte, Chicago, N. L., 1908.
992—Bris. Lord, Cleveland, A. L., 1909.
992—John Collins, Chicago, A. L., 1917.
992—Babe Ruth, Boston, A. L., 1919.

Most Chances Per Season
478—Sam Rice, Washington, A. L., 1920.
468—Max Carey, Pittsburg, N. L., 1917.

Most Chances Per Game
13—Charles Shorten, Providence, I. L., June 14, 1915.
12—Oscar Felsch, Chicago, A. L., June 23, 1919.
11—George Shafer, Boston, N. L., Sept. 26, 1877.

11—Joe Hornung, Boston, N. L., Sept. 23, 1881.

11—Dick Harley, St. Louis, N. L., June 30, 1898.

11—Topsy Hartzel, Chicago, N. L., Sept. 10, 1901.

Most Put-outs Per Season

454—Sam Rice, Washington, A. L., 1920.

440—Max Carey, Pittsburg, N. L., 1917.

Most Put-outs Per Game

11—Dick Harley, St. Louis, N. L., June 30, 1898.

11—Topsy Hartzel, Chicago, N. L., Sept. 10, 1901.

11—Oscar Felsch, Chicago, A. L., June 23, 1919.

Most Assists Per Season

39—Harry Niles, St. Louis, A. L., 1906.

39—Mike Mitchell, Cincinnati, N. L., 1907.

Most Assists Per Game

4—William Crowley, Buffalo, N. L., Aug. 27, 1880.

4—Charles Millar, Cincinnati, N. L., May 30, 1895.

4—William Holms, Chicago, N. L., Aug. 21, 1903.

4—Fred Clarke, Pittsburg, N. L., Aug. 23, 1910.

4—Oscar Felsch, Chicago, A. L., Aug. 14, 1919.

Most Errors Per Season

47—George Van Haltren, Baltimore, N. L., 1893.

26—Jess Burkett, St. Louis, A. L., 1902.

Most Errors Per Game
5—Mike Dorgan, New York, N. L., May 24, 1884.

5—Al Selbach, Baltimore, A. L., Aug. 19, 1902.

No Errors Per Season
Jos. Schrall, playing the outfield for Syracuse, New York State League, season of 1908 had the following record:

Games	Put-outs	Assists	Errors	Per Cent.
131	155	17	0	1.000

WORLD'S RECORDS OF CATCHERS
Highest Fielding Average Per Season
990—Joe Sugden, St. Louis, A. L., 1904.

990—Jack O'Connor, St. Louis, A. L., 1906.

990—Frank Bowerman, New York, N. L., 1907.

990—George Gibson, Pittsburg, N. L., 1912.

990—Fred Cody, Boston, A. L., 1912.

990—Bert Whaling, Boston, N. L., 1913.

990—R. Perkins, Athletics, A. L., 1918.

Most Games Caught in Succession
155—Henry Cote, Grand Rapids, Inter-State League, 1898.

140—George Gibson, Pittsburg, N. L., 1909.

100—Steve O'Neil, Cleveland, A. L., 1920.

Most Years Catching 100 or More Games
8—Ray Schalk, Chicago, A. L.

6—George Gibson, Pittsburg, N. L.

Most Years Catching 100 or More Consecutive Games

8—Ray Schalk, Chicago, A. L.

6—John Meyers, New York, N. L.

Most Chances Accepted in Season

984—Kearns, Dallas, Texas League, 1907.

947—Rariden, Newark, Federal League, 1915.

924—Street, Washington, A. L., 1909.

847—Gibson, Pittsburg, N. L., 1909.

Most Chances Accepted in Game

23—Robert Bagnall, Milwaukee, Union Association, Oct. 7, 1884.

22—Vincent Nava, Providence, N. L., June 7, 1884.

19—O. Schreckengost, Athletics, A. L., May 15, 1903.

18—Ed. Sweeney, New York, A. L., July 10, 1912.

Most Put-outs Per Season

785—O. Schreckengost, Athletics, 1903.

729—John Meyers, New York, N. L., 1911.

Most Put-outs in One Game (Nine Innings)

23—Chas. Bennett, Detroit, N. L., Sept. 26, 1884.

19—Vincent Nava, Providence, N. L., June 7, 1884.

18—Schreckengost, Philadelphia, A. L., May 15, 1903.

16—Herb. Ruel, New York, A. L., Sept. 27, 1919.

Most Assists Per Season

243—Noyce, Hutchinson, W. L., 1906 (116 games).

214—Pat Moran, Boston, N. L., 1903.

212—O. Stanage, Detroit, A. L., 1911.

129—R. W. Schalk, Chicago, A. L., 1921.

120—Walter Schmidt, Pittsburg, N. L., 1921.

Most Assists Per Game

11—Frank Flint, Chicago, N. L., July 29, 1884.

11—Ed. Sweeney, New York, A. L., July 10, 1912.

Most Errors Per Season

81—Emil Gross, Philadelphia, N. L., 1880.

41—Oscar Stanage, Detroit, A. L., 1911.

Most Errors Per Game

8—Emil Gross, Philadephia, N. L., Aug. 21, 1883.

4—Ira Thomas, New York, A. L., Aug. 18, 1907.

4—J. Peters, Cleveland, A. L., May 16, 1918.

Most Passed Balls in Season

31—George Gibson, Pittsburg, N. L., 1906.

25—John Henry, Washington, A. L., 1911.

Greatest Number Games Caught in Succession

155—Henry Cote, Grand Rapids, Int. State L., 1898.

140—George Gibson, Pittsburg, N. L., 1909.

Greatest Number of Games Caught—Season

155—Henry Cote, Grand Rapids, Int. State L., 1898.

151—Ray Schalk, Chicago, A. L., 1920.

150—Geo. Gibson, Pittsburg, N. L., 1909.

142—Snyder, St. Louis, N. L., 1915.

139—Severied, St. Louis, 1917.

139—Roger Bresnahan, New York, N. L., 1908.

WORLD'S RECORDS IN BASEBALL HITTING

The Charlotte Club, South Atlantic League, in the fourth inning with Winston-Salem in Piedmont League, made this record. First three men hit the first three balls safely, and O'Connell, shortstop, hit fourth ball pitched for a home run. Four balls pitched, four hits, four runs. (April 14, 1921.)

Most Hits Per Season

Clubs

1995—St. Louis, A. A., 1887.

1782—Philadelphia, N. L., 1894.

1724—Detroit, A. L., 1921.

Players

257—Geo. H. Sisler, St. Louis, A. L., 1920.

243—Wm. Keeler, Baltimore, N. L., 1897.

Most Hits Per Game

8—Arlie Latham, Cincinnati, N. L., June 18, 1893.

8—John McPhee, Cincinnati, N. L., June 18, 1893.

8—Fred Tenney, Boston, N. L., May 31, 1897.

8—Bill McCormick, Chicago, N. L., June 20, 1897.

Most Hits Per Game—Minor League

8—Jack Glasscock, St. Paul, A. A., 1896.

8—"Nig" Clarke, Corsicana, Texas L., 1902.

8—Alexander, Corsicana, Texas L., 1902.

8—Pendleton, Corsicana, Texas L., 1902.

Most Extra Bases in One Game

32—"Nig" Clarke, Corsicana, Texas L., July 14, 1902.

28—Harry Wright, Cincinnati, N. L., June 12, 1867.

24—"Lip" Pike, Athletics (Phila.), July 16, 1866.

20—Al. Reach, Athletics (Phila.), Sept. 30, 1865.

19—McElvey, Minneapolis, A. A., April 10, 1911.

18—Geo. Kelly, Rochester, I. L., June 24, 1919.

18—Botenus, Buffalo, E. L., May 12, 1895.

17—Bob Lowe, Boston, N. L., May 30, 1905.

17—Ed. Delehanty, Phila., N. L., July 13, 1906.

17—Jackley, Ironton, O., Sept. 9, 1913.

17—Jack Crooks, Omaha, W. L., June 8, 1889.

16—Lave Cross, Philadelphia, N. L., May 28, 1893.

16—Jack Cronin, Pawtucket, May 31, 1892.

16—Muldoon, Cleveland, N. L., Aug. 18, 1882.

Most Total Bases in Game

17—Bob Lowe, Boston, N. L., May 30, 1894.

17—Ed. Delehanty, Philadelphia, N. L., July 13, 1896.

13—Ed. Gharrity, Washington, A. L., June 23, 1919.

Most Extra Base Hits—Season
Clubs

466—Boston, N. L., 1894.

454—New York, A. L., 1920.

Players

216—Geo. "Babe" Ruth, New York, A. L., 1920.

147—Sam Thompson, Philadelphia, N. L., 1895.

147—John Freeman, Washington, N. L., 1899.

Most Sacrifice Hits—Season
Club

392—Boston, A. A., 1891.

361—Philadelphia, N. L., 1890.

310—Boston, A. L., 1917.

Player

67—Ray Chapman, Cleveland, A. L., 1917.

67—Ed. Burke, New York, N. L., 1893.

Most Sacrifice Hits—Game

4—Wade Killifer, Washington, A. L., 1910.

4—Jake Daubert, Brooklyn, N. L., 1914.

4—Jack Barry, Boston, A. L., 1916.

4—Ray Chapman, Cleveland, A. L., 1917.

Most Sacrifice Flies—Season
Club

66—New York, N. L., 1912.

63—Boston, A. L., 1915.

Player

16—Joe Tinker, Chicago, N. L., 1912.

16—Sam Crawford, Detroit, A. L., 1914.

16—Charles Gandil, Washington, A. L., 1914.

Most Sacrifice Flies—Game

3—Henry Steinfeldt, Chicago, N. L., 1909.

Most Two Base Hits Made—Game

4—Tom Tucker, Boston, N. L., 1893.

4—Joe Kelley, Baltimore, N. L., 1894.

4—Ed. Delehanty, Philadelphia, N. L., 1894.

4—Frank Dillon, Detroit, A. L., 1901.

4—Tris Speaker, Boston, A. L., 1912.

4—Frank Isbell, Chicago, A. L., 1906 (World's Series).

4—Sherry Magee, Philadelphia, N. L., 1914.

4—C. C. Cravath, Philadelphia, N. L., 1915.

Most Two Base Hits Per Inning
2—Bob Byrne, Pittsburg, N. L., 1913.
2—Hal. Janvrin, Boston, A. L., 1914.
2—John Collins, Chicago, A. L., 19'.6.
2—William Gardner, Boston, A. L., 1917.
2—Oscar Felsch, Chicago, A. L., 1917.
2—Ed. Roush, Cincinnati, N. L., 1919.

Most Three Base Hits Made in Career
253—Hans Wagner, Pittsburg, N. L.
250—Sam Crawford, Detroit, A. L.

Most Three Base Hits—Season
Club
148—Philadelphia, N. L., 1894.
148—Baltimore, N. L., 1894.
Player
36—Owen Wilson, Pittsburg, N. L., 1912.
26—Joe Jackson, Cleveland, A. L., 1912.
26—Sam Crawford, Detroit, A. L., 1914.

Most Three Base Hits Made Per Game
4—George Strief, Philadelphia, A. A., 1885.
4—William Joyce, New York, N. L., 1897.

Most Two Base Hits Made in Season
Club
355—Cleveland, A. L., 1921.
Player
56—Ed. Delehanty, Philadelphia, N. L., 1899.
52—Tris Speaker, Cleveland, A. L., 1921.

Most Two Base Hits Ever Made in Career

648—Hans Wagner, Pittsburg, N. L.

Most Two Base Hits Made in Game

14—Chicago, N. L., 1883.

Most Times at Bat—Season

Club

5495—St. Louis, N. L., 1920.

5465—Philadelphia, A. L., 1921.

Player

671—J. T. Tobin, St. Louis, A. L., 1921.

653—Bill Brown, Louisville, N. L., 1893.

Most Home Runs Made in Inning

2—Chas. Jones, Buffalo, N. L., June 10, 1880.

2—Link Lowe, Boston, N. L., May 30, 1894.

2—C. Fitzgerald, Wilkesbarre, N. Y. State L., June 27, 1889.

Most Home Runs Made in Career

162—"Babe" Ruth, New York, A. L.

117—C. C. Cravath, Philadelphia, N. L.

Greatest Number Home Runs in One Game

Clubs

25—Athletics, Philadelphia vs. Nationals J. C., Sept. 30, 1865.

19—Athletics, Philadelphia vs. Newcastle, Del., May 9, 1866.

19—Corsicana, Texas League, July 14, 1902.

9—Boston, N. L., vs. Cincinnati, N. L., May 30, 1904.

7—Detroit, N. L., vs. St. Louis, N. L., June 12, 1886.

6—Peoria vs. Quincy, July 2, 1890.

5—Washington, N. L. vs. Boston, N. L., Oct. 5, 1887.

Players

8—"Nig" Clarke, Corsicana, Texas L., July 14, 1902.

7—Harry Wright, Cincinnati, N. L., June 12, 1867.

6—"Lip" Pike, Philadelphia Athletics, July 16, 1866.

5—Al. Reach, Philadelphia Athletics, Sept. 30, 1865.

4—Muldoon, Cleveland, N. L., Aug. 18, 1882.

4—Crooks, Omaha, June 8, 1889.

4—Botenus, Buffalo, May 12, 1895.

4—Cronin, Pawtucket, May 31, 1892.

4—Lave Cross, Philadelphia, N. L., April 16, 1895.

4—McElvey, Minneapolis, A. L., April 10, 1911.

4—Ed. Delehanty, Philadelphia, N. L., July 13, 1906.

4—Bob Lowe, Boston, N. L., May 30, 1905.

4—Geo. Kelly, Rochester, Int. L., June 24, 1919.

4—Jackley, Ironton, O., Sept. 9, 1913.

Most Home Runs in Season

59—"Babe" Ruth, New York, A. L., 1921.

45—Perry Werden, Minneapolis, A. L., 1893.

Most Runs Batted in Game
11—Wilbert Robinson, Baltimore, N. L., 1892.

Most Runs Batted—Season
170—"Babe" Ruth, New York, A. L., 1921.
129—C. C. Cravath, Philadelphia, N. L., 1913.

Consecutive Hits in Consecutive Games
69—Joe Wilholt, Wichita, W. L., 1919.
44—William Keeler, Baltimore, N. L., 1897.
40—Tyrus A. Cobb, Detroit, A. L., 1911.

Most Extra Bases in One Inning
8—Tom Burns, Chicago, N. L., (H. R. and 2 Doubles) Sept. 6, 1883.
8—L. Robinson, Saginaw, O. S. L. (2 Triples, 1 Double), April 21, 1883.

World's Home Run Record—Season
Twenty-five or More
59—"Babe" Ruth, New York, A. L., 1921.
45—Werden, Minneapolis, 1893.
43—Calvert, Muskogee, 1917.
41—Yaryan, Wichita, 1920.
36—Roth, Evansville, 1901.
34—Beese, McAllester, W. A., 1916.
33—Sheely, Salt Lake City, 1920.
30—Bodie, San Francisco, 1910.
30—Beck, Wichita, 1920.
29—Cravath, Minneapolis, 1911.
27—Willamson, Chicago, N. L., 1884.

27—Bues, Seattle, 1911.

27—Mann, Seattle, 1912.

25—Freeman, Washington, N. L., 1899.

Home Runs in Succession

Shaffer, White, Rowe, Buffalo, N. L., Sept. 11, 1883.

Brouthers, Thompson, Rowe, Detroit, N. L. July 12, 1886.

Connor, Quinn, Ely, St. Louis, N. L., May 10, 1894.

Lajoie, Hickman, Bradley, Cleveland, A. L., June 30, 1902.

Delehanty, Coughlin, Carey, Washington, A. L., July 2, 1902.

Camnitz, Campbell, Clarke, Pittsburg, N. L., Aug. 22, 1910.

Zimmerman, Erwin, Wheat, Brooklyn, N. L., Aug. 3, 1911.

Peckinpaugh, Baker, Bodie, New York, A. L., July 4, 1919, A. M.

Homers in Consecutive Games

Munn of the Richmond, Blue Grass League, in 1912 made one home run in seven consecutive games.

Home Runs in Successive Days

4—Bradley, Cleveland, A. L., May 21, 22, 23, 24, 1912.

4—Ruth, New York, A. L., June 2, 3, 4, 5, 1918.

Baseball Records Held by Ruth
Hitting

Ruth has yet to make two home runs in one inning. But he already holds records aplenty as follows:

Fifty-nine home runs for a season.

Seven home runs in five successive games.

Three home runs in three successive times at bat, June 13 and 14, 1921.

One hundred and sixty-two home runs for his major league career.

Greatest number of home runs with bases filled in one season—Four, in 1919.

Eight games in which he hit two home runs—in 1920.

Greatest number of home runs hit off any pitcher by one man—10, off Dauss.

Greatest number of runs batted in one season, 170 (1921).

Most Home Runs Made in Game
9—Chicago, N. L., 5; Cincinnati, N. L., 4; 1895 (Game called in seventh inning).

Most Extra Base Hits in Career
996—Hans Wagner, Pittsburg, N. L.

Most Errors—Season
906—Buffalo, N. L., 1885.

Most Double Plays—Season
155—New York, N. L., 1921.
155—Chicago, A. L., 1921.

Most Hits Made in Game
36—Philadelphia, N. L., 1894.

Greatest Total Hits in Game
54—Cincinnati, N. L., 1893.

Most Base Hits in Career
3430—Hans Wagner, Pittsburg, N. L.

Most Consecutive Years of Hitting .300 or More
17—Hans Wagner, Pittsburg, N. L.

16—Tyrus R. Cobb, Detroit, A. L.

Batters Who Hit .300 and Over for Ten or More Consecutive Years
17—Wagner, Pittsburg.

16—Cobb, Detroit.

15—Anson, Chicago.

14—Brouthers, Buffalo-Detroit.

14—Keeler, Baltimore-Brooklyn.

12—Hamilton, Philadelphia-Boston.

12—Delehanty, Philadelphia.

11—Jackson, Cleveland-Chicago.

11—Lajoie, Philadelphia-Cleveland.

11—Joe Kelley, Baltimore.

10—Duffy, Boston.

10—Speaker, Boston-Cleveland.

10—Burkett, Cleveland-St. Louis.

Most Times a .300 Hitter
20—Adrian C. Anson, Chicago, N. L.

16—Tyrus R. Cobb, Detroit, A. L.

Most Consecutive Years Leading Batsman
9—Tyrus R. Cobb, Detroit, A. L., 1907-15.
4—Hans Wagner, Pittsburg, N. L., 1906-09.

Highest Batting Average for Club—Season
343—Philadelphia, N. L., 1894.
316—Detroit, A. L., 1921.
308—St. Louis, N. L., 1921.
308—St. Louis, A. L., 1920.

Most One-Base Hits in Career
2432—Hans Wagner, Pittsburg, N. L.

Most Extra Bases on Hits—Season
861—New York Americans, 1921.

Greatest Total Bases on Hits
2425—Boston, N. L., 1894.

Most Put-outs Per Season
4396—Cleveland, A. L., 1910.
4359—Philadelphia, N. L., 1913.

Highest Batting Average in Season
492—J. E. ("Tip") O'Neill, St. Louis, A. A., 1887.
438—Hugh Duffy, Boston, N. L., 1894.
420—Tyrus R. Cobb, Detroit, A. L., 1911.

Most Years 200 Hits or More
8—Willie Keeler, Baltimore-Brooklyn, N. L.

4—Tyrus R. Cobb, Detroit, A. L.

Four-Hundred Hitters

Few batters can claim honor of a batting average of 400 or better for a season; making 300 is the ambition of all players.

Jess Burkett holds the record, having been in the four hundred per cent class three seasons, 1895, 1896, and 1899. Players who batted 400 or better twice, are: Anson; Stovey; Thompson; Delehanty, and Cobb.

Here Is the Complete Record of "400" Hitters

Hugh Duffy, Boston, N. L., 1894—.438.

George Turner, Philadelphia, N. L., 1894—.432.

Jess Burkett, Cleveland, N. L., 1893—.423.

Jess Burkett, Cleveland, N. L., 1896—.410.

Jess Burkett, St. Louis, N. L., 1899—.402.

Joe Goodall, Louisville, A. A., 1890—.422.

"Ty" Cobb, Detroit, A. L., 1911—.420.

"Ty" Cobb, Detroit, A. L., 1912—.410.

Jake Stenzel, Pittsburg, N. L., 1893—.409.

Ed. Delehanty, Philadelphia, N. L., 1894—.400.

Ed. Delehanty, Philadelphia, N. L., 1899—.408.

Tom Esterbrook, Mets. A. A., 1884—.408.

Joe Jackson, Cleveland, A. L., 1911—.408.

A. C. Anson, Chicago, N. L., 1879—.407.

A. C. Anson, Chicago, N. L., 1887—.421.

George Sisler, St. Louis, A. L., 1920—.407.

Fred Clarke, Louisville, N. L., 1897—.406.

Larry Lajoie, Athletics, A. L., 1901—.405.

Charles Farrell, Boston, A. L., 1903—.404.
Harry Stovey, Athletics, A. A., 1884—.404.
Harry Stovey, Athletics, A. A., 1887—.402.
Ross Barnes, Chicago, N. L., 1876—.403.
Sam Thompson, Detroit, N. L., 1887—.406.
Sam Thompson, Detroit, N. L., 1894—.403.

Records Made in 1887

In 1887 players were allowed four strikes: A base on balls counted as a base hit, consequently batting averages of that season should not be compared with those of other seasons, as only three strikes are allowed and a "walk" is not credited as a hit.

"Tip" O'Neill, who played the outfield for St. Louis, American Association, made the wonderful record of .492 during 1887. He is credited with 277 hits in 123 games.

Records of this season are separated, and should be borne in mind when speaking of the wonderful batters in the "good old days." Here they are:

J. E. "Tip" O'Neill, St. Louis, A. A., 1887—.492.
Pete Browning, Louisville, A. A., 1887—.471.
Denny Lyons, Athletics, A. A., 1887—.469.
Bob Carruthers, St. Louis, A. A., 1887—.459.
Al. Maul, Philadelphia, N. L., 1887—.450.
Willie Keeler, Baltimore, N. L., 1887—.432.
Bill Robinson, St. Louis, A. A., 1887—.426.
A. C. Anson, Chicago, N. L., 1887—.421.
Dan Brouthers, Detroit, N. L., 1887—.419.

Charles Ferguson, Philadelphia, N. L., 1887—.412.

Del. Darling, Chicago, N. L., 1887—.411.

Denny Mack, Louisville, A. A., 1887—.410.

Sam Thompson, Detroit, N. L., 1887—.406.

Paul Radford, Mets. N. Y., A. A., 1887—.404.

Dave Orr, Mets. N. Y., A. A., 1887—.403.

Harry Stovey, Athletics, A. A., 1887—.402.

Tom Burns, Baltimore, A. A., 1887—.401.

Ed. Burch, Brooklyn, A. A., 1887—.400.

National Association B. B. C.
George Wright, Boston, 1873—.422.

Jas. White, Boston, 1872—.401.

Unassisted Triple Plays
Individuals

Harry O'Hagen (F. B.), Rochester M. E. L. vs. Jersey City, Aug. 18, 1902.

Frank Eutice (T. B.), Pottsville, Pa. vs. Lebanon, Pa., Sept. 2, 1902.

William McGuire (S. S.), Hoquiam vs. Portland, Cal., Sept. 6, 1902.

Ralph Frary (S. S.), Seattle vs. Tacoma, May 16, 1906.

Larry Schaffley (S. B.), Portland vs. Seattle, June 10, 1906.

Simeon Murch (S. B.), Manchester vs. New Bedford, Sept. 6, 1905.

Jack O'Neill (S. S.), Hannibal vs. Moberly, June 28, 1908.

James Decker (F. B.), Richfield, Pa., vs. Beaver Springs, Pa., Aug. 17, 1908.

Red Hinton (T. B.), Dayton, O., vs. Tippecanoe , O., (Amateur Team), April 15, 1909.

Neal Ball, (S. B.), Cleveland, A. L., vs. Boston, A. L., May 19, 1909.

Charles Dineen (T. B.), Lymansville vs. Kirby's Same Town, June 19, 1910.

Harry Calvert (T. B.), Oregon vs. Woodburn Club, July 30, 1911.

Walter Carlisle (C. F.), Vernon vs. Los Angeles, July 19, 1911.

George Smith (S. B.), Bratz All Stars, Buffalo, vs. Pierce Arrows, May 7, 1912.

Roy Alken (T. B.), Waco vs. Houston, May 9, 1912.

John Foreman (S. S.), Kankakee vs. Champaign, July 15, 1912.

William Rapps (F. B.), Portland vs. Oakland, Sept. 14, 1912.

Phil. Cooney (S. B.), Omaha vs. Denver, July 5, 1917.

Harry Knaupp (S. B.), New Orleans vs. Chattanooga, Aug. 9, 1916.

Walter Keating, (S. S.), Buffalo vs. Akron, Aug. 31, 1920.

William Wambsganss (S. B.), Cleveland, A. L., vs. Brooklyn, N. L., Oct. 10, 1920 (World's Series).

Geo. Smiley, Knoxville (C. F.), Knoxville, April 25, 1921.

Heinie Sands (S. S.), Salt Lake City vs. Sacramento, July 4, 1921.

Clubs Making Triple Plays

Two triple plays have been made but once in a single game. Once between Butte and Los Angeles on April 23, 1903, when Reilly, Hollingsworth and Messerly made the first, and Reilly to Messerly the second.

In a game between Kansas City and Toledo, on June 14, 1904, Loewe and Sullivan made the first, while Loewe and Ryan made the second.

April 24, 1911, when Battle Creek and Grand Rapids played, Battle Creek made two triple plays against Grand Rapids.

Most Games Played Consecutively
678—Everett Scott, Boston, A. L., 1916-1920.
578—Geo. Pinckney, Brooklyn, St. Louis, N. L., 1885-1900.

Most Times Batter Faced Pitchers
10238—Hans Wagner, Pittsburg, N. L., 21 years.
7774—Ty Cobb, Detroit, A. L., 16 years.

Most Runs Per Season
Club
1221—Boston, N. L., 1894.
948—New York, A. L., 1921.

Player
196—Billy Hamilton, Philadelphia, N. L., 1894.
177—Geo. "Babe" Ruth, New York, A. L., 1921.

Most Runs Scored in Career

1750—Hans Wagner, Pittsburg, N. L.

1631—Ty Cobb, Detroit, A. L.

Most Home Runs by Pinch Hitter

3—Ham Hyatt, Pittsburg, N. L., 1913.

1—Ham Hyatt, Pittsburg, N. L., 1914.

Most Assists in Game
Club

33—Des Moines, Western League, Aug. 8, 1921.

28—Los Angeles, P. C. L., Aug. 28, 1917.

27—Brooklyn, N. L., June 14, 1906.

27—Boston, N. L., June 30, 1919.

Most Assists in Season
Club

2446—Chicago, A. L., 1907.

2349—New York, N. L., 1888.

Least Assists Per Game
Clubs

1—Laporte Reserves vs. New Carlisle, Ind., 1914.

1—Chicago, A. L., (Weaver made assist), May 19, 1917.

Players

2—New York vs. Pittsburg, N. L., (McGinnity, Pitcher, got both), 1906.

2—Pittsburg vs. Philadelphia, N. L., (Voix, Shortstop, got both), 1915.

2—Athletics vs. Cincinnati, A. A. (Knight, Outfielder, got both), 1884.

Most Assists in One Game by Outfielder

6—Paul Hines (C. F.), Chicago, N. L., July 29, 1876.

Most Stolen Bases Per Inning

8—Washington vs. Cleveland, A. L., July 19, 1915.

Most Stolen Bases Per Game

Clubs

17—New York, N. L., 1890.

Players

7—Wm. Hamilton, Philadelphia, N. L., vs. Washington, Aug. 31, 1894.

7—Geo. Gore, Chicago vs. Providence, N. L., June 25, 1881.

6—E. T. Collins, Athletics vs. St. Louis, A. L., Sept. 11, 1912.

6—E. T. Collins, Athletics vs. St. Louis, A. L., Sept. 22, 1912.

Most Bases Stolen Per Season

Clubs

423—New York, N. L., 1887.
288—Washington, A. L., 1913.

Players

156—Harry Stovey, Athletics, Philadelphia, A. A., 1888.

136—Harry Stovey, Athletics, Philadelphia, A. A., 1890.

115—Wm. Hamilton, Philadelphia, N. L., 1891.

96—Tyrus R. Cobb, Detroit, A. L., 1915.

Most Stolen Bases by Player in Career
796—Tyrus R. Cobb, Detroit, A. L.

717—Hans Wagner, Pittsburg, N. L.

Highest Percentage of Games Won
.798—Chicago, N. L., 1880.

.691—Boston, A. L., 1912.

Lowest
.235—Athletics, A. L., 1916.

.130—Cleveland, N. L., 1899.

Most No-Hit Games Per Season
5—American League, 1917.

4—National League, 1880.

4—National League, 1898.

Most One-Hit Games Per Season
13—National League, 1910.

12—American League, 1906.

Most Two-Hit Games Per Season
28—American League, 1910.

26—National League, 1915.

Most Three-Hit Games Per Season
56—American League, 1909.

51—National League, 1905.

Greatest Number of Shutouts—Season
164—National League, 1908.
145—American League, 1909.

Greatest Number of 1-0 Games—Season
43—National League, 1907.
41—American League, 1908.

Greatest Number of Victories—Season
116—Chicago, N. L., 1906.
105—Boston, A. L., 1912.

Greatest Number of Defeats—Season
134—Cleveland, N. L., 1899.
117—Athletics, A. L., 1916.

Greatest Number of Games Won Abroad— Consecutively
17—New York, N. L., 1916.
16—Washington, A. L., 1912.

World's Record Shut Out Games
37-0—Philadelphia, A. A., vs. Philadelphia, N. L., April 11, 1882.
28-0—Providence vs. Philadelphia, N. L., Aug. 21, 1883.
20-0—New York vs. Washington, A. L., (6 innings).

World's Record Largest Scores
209-10—Buffalo vs. Columbus, June 8, 1869.

162-11—Athletics vs. Danville, P. M., Oct. 20, 1865.

101-8—Athletics vs. Williamsport, A. M., Oct. 20, 1865.

157-1—Chicago vs. Memphis, May 13, 1870.

132-1—Cleveland vs. Amateurs, May 17, 1870 (5 innings).

114-2—Athletics vs. Nationals, Sept. 30, 1865.

38-1—Mutuals vs. Chicago, June 18, 1874.

51-48—Atlantics, Brooklyn vs. Athletics, Philadelphia, July 5, 1869.

49-0—Dartmouth College vs. Middlebury, June 16, 1882.

Record 100 Yard Dash by League Players

10 Seconds, Hans Lobert, Cincinnati, N. L., Oct. 10, 1910.

10 Seconds, Max Carey, Pittsburg, N. L., Oct. 1, 1916.

World's Record Circling Bases

13 4/5 Seconds, Hans Lobert, Cincinnati, N. L., Oct. 10, 1910.

13 4/5 Seconds, Max Carey, Pittsburg, N. L., Oct. 1, 1916.

World's Record Longest Scoreless Games

25 Ins.—Grand Forks vs. Fargo, July 18, 1891.

22 Ins.—Burlington vs. Keokuk, C. A., June 27, 1915.

22 Ins.—Hannibal vs. Rock Island, 3 Eye League, July 10, 1916.

21 Ins.—Lincoln vs. Joplin, W. L., Aug. 12, 1917.

20 Ins.—Pittsburg vs. Boston, N. L., Aug. 1, 1918.

18 Ins.—Detroit vs. Washington, A. L., July 16, 1909.

World's Record Longest Games

30 Ins.—Brooklyn A. C. vs. East End Stars, July 4, 1907.

26 Ins.—Decatur vs. Bloomington.

26 Ins.—Dixon vs. Muscatine, June 25, 1909.

26 Ins.—Boston vs. Brooklyn, N. L., May 1, 1920.

24 Ins.—Boston vs. Philadelphia, A. L., Sept. 1, 1906.

Greatest Number Tie Games—Season

19—American League, 1910.

16—National League, 1913.

Greatest Number Extra Inning Games—Season

80—American League, 1916.

78—National League, 1916.

Greatest Number of Runs Scored in Game

43—National League. Chicago, 36; Louisville, 7.

29—American League. Detroit, 21; St. Louis, 8.

Greatest Winning Streaks
Clubs

27—Corsicana, Texas L., 1902.

26—New York, N. L., 1916.

25—Baltimore, Int. L., 1920.

19—Chicago, A. L., 1916.

Greatest Losing Streaks

Clubs

32—Austin, Texas League, 1914.

26—Louisville, A. A., 1898.

23—Pittsburg, N. L., 1890.

20—Boston, A. L., 1906.

20—Athletics, A. L., 1920.

World's Record Hitting

To make five or six hits in a game is heralded as phenomenal, but Wilbert Robinson, playing for Baltimore, and now managing the Brooklyns, made seven hits in one game against St. Louis on June 10, 1892. This performance is all the more remarkable when we note that the pitchers vere none other than "Cy" Young, Theodore Breitenstein and "Pretzel" Getzein, three crackerjacks of those times.

On September 6, 1883, Tom Burns, Chicago third baseman against Detroit, was at bat three times in one inning, making a home run and two doubles. Burns made these hits in the seventh inning when Chicago scored 18 runs.

On April 21, 1883, Robinson, one of the players with Saginaw against Dayton, was at bat three times in the sixth inning, making two triples and a double. Saginaw made twenty (20) runs in that game.

Bill George in a game with St. Paul vs. Kansas City on June 21, 1896, was at bat twice in the sixth inning, making two home runs. The St. Paul team won. The winners made thirty-five hits for a total of fifty-six bases. Scored thirteen runs in the sixth.

In 1884 Captain A. C. Anson, of the Chicago N. L. Club, made five home runs in two games.

7 Hits—two home runs, three doubles, two singles in succession, a total of 16 bases by Hans Wagner, Pittsburg, N. L. Aug. 22, 1910.

8 Hits—Seven singles, one triple, Larry Lajoie, Cleveland, A. L., vs. St. Louis, Oct. 9, 1910.

Greatest Number of Hits Consecutively

11 safe hits, Tris Speaker, Cleveland, A. L., 1920.

10 safe hits, J. Gettman, Washington, N. L., 1899.

9 safe hits, "Doc" Johnston, Cleveland, A. L., 1919.

Memphis Club (Southern Assn.) defeated Little Rock, scoring 29 runs on 30 hits at Memphis, Tenn., Aug. 9, 1921. The previous minor league record was 24 runs made by Atlanta against Birmingham in 1920.

Sam Rice of Washington Holds World's Record of Outfield Chances

Sam Rice in 1920 placed the record for chances accepted at 478 against the old record by Max Carey of the Pirates, who in 1917 accepted 468 chances.

Brother Against Brother in World's Series Games

Since 1884, when the World's Series games were first played, there have been only two such series where brothers have played on opposing teams, once in 1920, when Jimmy Johnston of the Brooklyn team had his brother Wheeler "Doc" Johnston of the Cleveland team as his opponent; and in 1921 Bob Meusel of the New York Yanks opposed his brother Emil "Irish" Meusel of the New York Giants.

Longest Drive on Record

On June 14, 1921, Babe Ruth, in a game against St. Louis, made a hit that traveled 430 feet. This was his second home run into the center field bleachers. The hit was made on the Polo Grounds.

Some Home Runs

In a series between Philadelphia and Detroit, played in the former city, there were fifteen home runs made by the two teams, the Athletics cracking out ten of them. During the series, sixty-five runs scored in the four games. The ball was hit for 106 safeties for a grand total of 174 bases.

SIX HITS IN A GAME

Ed. Delehanty, One Major League Player, Did It Twice

O'Rourke Had Two Such Streaks in 1919

Ed. Delehanty is the only player in Major Leagues who made six hits in a game twice. The first time was with Cleveland Players League in 1890, and in 1894 with Philadelphia.

Only Player to Do it Twice in One Season

Frank O'Rourke, who formerly played with Toronto, now with Washington, is the only player who ever did it twice in one season. On the opening day of the International League Season, he made his first six hits, and in the latter part of the season he did it again.

Both Willie Keeler and Jack Doyle on the Baltimore, N. L. Club, made six hits each the same day, Sept. 3, 1897.

From 1902 when Jimmy Williams made six hits in a game with Baltimore until George Cutshaw of the Brooklyn team did it in 1915, no player made six hits in a game.

Here is the complete record of all players who have made six hits in a game, excepting season of 1887, when players had four strikes.

Six Hits Per Game

Lew Dickerson, Worcester, N. L., June 16, 1881.

Guy Hecker, Louisville, A. A., Aug. 15, 1886.

Jerry Denny, Indianapolis, N. L., May 4, 1889.

Larry Twitchell, Cleveland, N. L., Aug. 15, 1889.

Ed. Delehanty, Cleveland, P. L., June 2, 1890.

Jack Glasscock, New York, N. L., Sept. 27, 1890.

Bill Weaver, Louisville, A. A., Aug. 12, 1890.

Billy Shindle, Philadelphia, P. L., Aug. 26, 1890.

Ed. Delehanty, Philadelphia, N. L., June 16, 894.

Walter Brodie, Baltimore, N. L., July 9, 1894.

Charles Zimmer, Cleveland, N. L., July 11, 894.

Link Lowe, Boston, N. L., May 3, 1895.

George Davis, New York, N. L., Aug. 15, 1895.

Roger Connor, St. Louis, N. L., June 1, 1895.

Tom Tucker, Washington, N. L., July 15, 1897.

Willie Keeler, Baltimore, N. L., Sept. 3, 1897.

Jack Doyle, Baltimore, N. L., Sept. 3, 1897.

Clarence Beaumont, Pittsburg, N. L., July 22, 1899.

Chick Stahl, Boston, N. L., May 31, 1899.

Mike Donlin, Baltimore, A. L., June 24, 1901.

W. Nance, Detroit, A. L., July 13, 1901.

Harvey, Cleveland, A. L., April 25, 1902.

Dan Murphy, Athletics, A. L., July 8, 1902.

Jimmy Williams, Baltimore, A. L., Aug. 25, 1902.

George Cutshaw, Brooklyn, N. L., Aug. 9, 1915.

Dave Bancroft, New York, N. L., June 21, 1920.

A WONDERFUL PERFORMANCE BY GUY HECKER, WHICH PROBABLY WILL NEVER BE EQUALLED

The wonderful accomplishments in all-around baseball of such players as Sisler, Ruth, Lajoie, Wagner, Hornsby and others rightly excite our admiration. Compared with the record established by Guy Hecker—a star of the Eighties—they must necessarily take second place.

He Is Credited With—

having pitched a no-hit game, playing first base, in which position he was not offered a chance. He also has to his credit the remarkable record of having scored seven runs in a regular nine-inning game.

Hecker Scores Seven Runs

Louisville, Ky., August 16, 1886

Louisville

	AB	R	H	PO	A	E
Kerins, 1B	5	3	2	9	0	0
Hecker, P	7	7	6	0	0	0
Browning, LF	7	2	3	4	0	0
Gross, C	7	0	2	4	1	0
Werrick, 3B	4	1	0	1	2	0
Wolf, RF	6	1	1	0	0	1
White, SS	6	3	4	3	2	1
Mack, 2B	6	2	2	3	7	2
Sylvester, CF	5	3	3	3	0	0
Totals	52	22	23	27	12	4

Baltimore

	AB	R	H	PO	A	E
O'Connell, CF	4	1	0	6	0	0
Manning, RF	4	0	0	1	0	1
Mudloon, 2B	4	0	1	2	1	1
Sommers, LF	4	0	0	4	0	0
Davis, 3B	3	0	0	0	0	0
D. Conway, P	3	1	0	0	2	0
Scott, 1B	4	1	3	9	0	0
Maccullar, SS	4	1	1	1	3	0
W. Conway, C	4	1	0	4	1	1
Totals	34	5	4	27	7	5

Louisville	1	5	0	1	0	4	2	4	5—22
Baltimore	0	2	0	0	3	0	0	0	0— 5

Hecker Pitching a No-Hit Game

Pittsburg, Pa., September 19, 1882

Louisville

	R	H	PO	A	E
Browning, SS	1	0	1	5	3
Hecker, P	0	1	2	8	0
Sullivan, C	0	1	4	3	2
Wolf, RF	0	0	3	0	0
Mack, 2B	0	1	2	2	0
Mullane, 1B	1	0	11	0	0
Schenck, 3B	0	0	0	0	0
Maskrey, LF	0	0	3	0	0
Reccius, CF	1	0	1	0	2
Totals	3	3	27	18	7

Allegheny

	R	H	PO	A	E
Swartwood	1	0	0	1	0
Mansell	0	0	0	1	1
Taylor	0	0	3	0	0
Peters	0	0	0	8	0
Morgan	0	0	1	0	0
Battin	0	0	1	3	0
Strief	0	0	3	4	1
Lane	0	0	19	0	0
Driscoll	0	0	0	7	0
Totals	1	0	27	24	2

Louisville	0	0	0	0	0	2	1	0	0—3
Allegheny	0	0	0	0	0	1	0	0	0—1

No Put Out at First Base

Louisville, Ky., October 8, 1887

Louisville

	AB	R	H	PO	A	E
Mack, 2B	4	0	1	7	1	0
Browning, CF	4	0	1	2	0	1
Collins, LF	4	0	1	3	0	0
Kerins, C	4	0	2	9	2	0
White, SS	4	0	1	2	0	1
Werrick, 3B	4	0	2	0	2	1
Wolf, RF	4	0	0	1	0	0
Hecker, 1B	4	0	0	0	0	0
Ramsey, P	3	0	1	0	6	1
Totals	35	0	9	24	11	4

Cincinnati

	AB	R	H	PO	A	E
Nichol, RF	4	1	1	3	0	1
McPhee, 2B	4	0	1	2	3	1
Fennelly, SS	4	1	3	3	3	0
Reilly, 1B	4	0	0	10	0	0
Corkhill, CF	4	0	0	3	0 ·	0
Keenan, C	4	0	2	2	2	0
Tebeau, LF	3	0	0	3	1	0
Serad, P	3	0	0	0	2	0
Carpenter, 3B	3	0	1	1	3	0
	—	—	—	—	—	—
Totals	33	2	8	27	14	2

Louisville .....·...0 0 0 0 0 0 0 0 0—0
Cincinnati ....2 0 0 0 0 0 0 0 x—2

OUTFIELD ASSISTS RECORD SIX IN ONE GAME

No other Outfielder has a record of making six assists from Center Field as Paul Hines did on July 29, 1876, as a member of the Chicago White Stockings.

THE SCORE:

Chicago

	AB	R	H	PO	A	E
Barnes, 2B	6	3	2	3	5	0
Peters, SS	6	1	1	1	3	0
McVey, 1B	6	1	4	11	0	0
Anson, 3B	5	1	2	1	2	0
White, C	5	1	1	2	1	0

Hines, CF	5	1	2	6	6	0
Spalding, P	5	0	2	1	3	0
Andrus, RF	5	1	1	1	0	0
Glenn, LF	5	0	1	1	0	0
	—	—	—	—	—	
Totals	48	9	16	27	20	

Cincinnati

	AB	R	H	PO	A
Jones, CF	4	0	0	3	0
Booth, SS	4	0	0	1	4
Gould, 1B	4	0	2	13	0
Clack, 3B	4	0	0	1	4
Dean, P	3	1	1	0	3
Sweezy, 2B	3	0	0	1	4
Foley, C	3	1	1	4	0
Pearson, RF	4	0	1	2	0
Snyder, LF	3	0	2	2	0
	—	—	—	—	—
Totals	32	2	7	27	15

Chicago ....1 0 0 0 4 0 1 1 2—

Cincinnati ....0 0 1 0 1 0 0 0 0—

GAMES PLAYED IN RECORD TIME

Full Nine Innings

32 Minutes—Mobile vs. Atlanta, Sept. 19, 1916

33 Minutes—New York vs. Philadelphia, N. L. Oct. 2, 1913.

36 Minutes—McAlester vs. Ardmore, Western A., Aug. 29, 1917.

40 Minutes—Reach All Americans vs. Tokio, apan, Nov. 27, 1909.

42 Minutes—Nashville vs. New Orleans, Sept. 7, 1910.

42 Minutes—Binghamton vs. Albany, Sept. 7, 912.

44 Minutes—Atlanta vs. Shreveport, Sept. 24, 904.

47 Minutes—Dayton vs. Ironton, O., Sept. 19, 884.

47 Minutes—San Francisco vs. Oakland, Nov. 9, 393.

46 Minutes—Los Angeles vs. Oakland, July 30, 905.

49 Minutes—Knoxville vs. Atlanta, Sept. 18, 902.

50 Minutes—San Francisco vs. Oakland, Aug. 3, 1893.

51 Minutes—Los Angeles vs. Oakland, July 30, 903.

51 Minutes—New York vs. Philadelphia, Sept. 3, 1917.

53 Minutes—Toledo vs. Columbus, Sept. 30, 911.

55 Minutes—Brooklyn vs. Cincinnati, N. L., ept. 21, 1919.

57 Minutes—Providence vs. Albany, Sept. 14, 393.

57 Minutes—Richmond vs. Frankport, Sept. 3, 911.

59 Minutes—Crookston vs. Fargo, Sept. 12, 907.

DOUBLE HEADERS

1 Hr. 45 Min.—Harrisburg vs. York. First Game, 48 Minutes. Second Game, 57 Minutes, Sept. 4, 1912.

1 Hr. 38½ Min.—Los Angeles vs. Oakland. First Game, 47½ Minutes. Second Game, 51 Minutes. July 30, 1905.

SLOW GAMES

July 30, 1862, it required four hours to score 12 runs between the Unions of Morrisania and Eckfords of Green Point to play a game.

A game played at Carrolton, Ky., on July 18, 1863, between two picked teams, started at ten o'clock in the morning, and was called on account of darkness at six P. M. with only seven innings played. The score was a tie with 58 runs each.

THREE EXCEPTIONAL RECORDS

Once in the history of Baseball have two clubs from two leading Baseball Leagues captured the pennants (Chicago), and the same year two other clubs (Boston) in the same city finished last.

In 1920 two batters from the same city in two leagues led the other players in batting.

Here Are the Records

Pennant Winners

1906—Chicago Cubs, won 116; lost 36—.763
1906—Chicago Sox, won, 93; lost 58—.616

Finished Last

1906—Boston Braves, won 49; lost 102—.323

1906—Boston Red Sox, won 49; lost 105—.318

Champion Batters

1920—Sisler, St. Louis, A. L., Hits, 257; Average .407.

1920—Hornsby, St. Louis, N. L., Hits, 218; Average, .370.

First Double Header in Major League
Sept. 18, 1883

First Game—Cleveland 5, Philadelphia 3.

Second Game—Cleveland 5, Philadelphia 1.

Three Games in a Day
July 4, 1878

First Game at New Bedford, New Bedford 15, Hartford 1.

Second Game at Taunton, New Bedford 3, Hartford 1.

Third Game at Providence, New Bedford 18, Hartford 3.

Four Games in a Day
Sept. 15, 1896

Sioux City and St. Joseph of the Western League. Sioux City winning all of them.

Six Games in a Day
Sept. 4, 1889

Manchester defeated Portland six games. Two played in the morning, four in the afternoon. Last game was forfeited in second inning.

First Time Three Games Were Played in Major League

Sept. 1, 1890

Brooklyn defeated Pittsburg three games.

First Game, Brooklyn 10, Pittsburg 9, A. M.

Second Game, Brooklyn 3, Pittsburg 2, P. M.

Third Game, Brooklyn 8, Pittsburg 4, P. M.

Greatest Number Consecutive Innings in Consecutive Games

1915

Washington 5	Chicago	6	13 Innings	Aug.	24
Washington 7	Chicago	4	14 Innings	Aug.	25
Washington 2	Chicago	1	13 Innings	Aug.	26
Washington 3	St. Louis	1	9 Innings	Aug.	27
Washington 1	St. Louis	2	12 Innings	Aug.	28
Washington 1	St. Louis	2	9 Innings	Aug.	29
Washington 4	New York	1	9 Innings	Aug.	31
Washington 3	New York	2	11 Innings	Aug.	31
Washington 2	New York	1	12 Innings	Sept.	1
Totals ..28		20	102		9

Record of First Shut-Out Game

Chicago vs. St. Louis, May 5th, 1876; Score, 1-0.

Record of First Uniforms Worn

Knickerbockers vs. Washington Club, June 3, 1851.

Record First Extra-Inning Game

10 Innings, Knickerbockers vs. Washington, June 17, 1851.

World's Record Big League Umpire
28 Years
Robert Emslie.

World's Record Attendance—Baseball
Game
42,620—Boston vs. Brooklyn. World's Series at Boston, Oct. 12, 1916.
Series
269,976—New York Americans vs. New York Nationals, 1921.

World's Record Admission to Game
$119,007—New York Americans vs. New York Nationals, Oct. 7, 1921.

World's Record Admission to Series
$900,233—New York Nationals vs. New York Americans, World Series, 1921.

World's Record Admission—Boxing
Dempsey vs. Carpentier, $1,600,000, July 4, 1921
Dempsey vs. Willard, $452,522, July 4, 1919
Johnson vs. Jeffries, $270,755, July 4, 1910.

World's Record Attendance
96,852—Six-day Bicycle Race, Madison Square Garden, 1921

WORLD'S RECORDS OF RUNNING HORSES
¼ mile, Bob Wade, Aug. 20, 1890; .21¼.
½ mile, Man o' War, May 29, 1920; .45 4/5.

4½ furlongs, Preceptor, May 19, 1908; .51.

⅝ mile, Maid Marian, Oct. 9, 1894; .56¾.

5½ furlongs, Plater, Oct. 21, 1902; 1.02 2/5

¾ mile, Artful, Oct. 15, 1904; 1.08.

6½ furlongs, Lady Vera, Oct. 19, 1906; 1.16 3/5.

⅞ mile, Paris, Sept. 12, 1914; 1.22 2/5.

1 mile (st.), Caimen, July 13, 1900; 1.33 1/5 (Eng.).

1 mile (Cir.) Sun Briar, Sept. 12, 1918; 1.34.

1 mile (St.) ⎰ Salvator, Aug. 28, 1890; 1.35½ America.
⎱ Froglegs, May 13, 1913; 1.39.

1 mile 20 yd., Sen. James, Feb. 15, 1918; 1.39.

1 mile 40 yds., ⎰ Preen, June 16, 1906; 1.42.
Mainchance, June 29, 1907; 1.42.
Harry Shaw, Nov. 9, 1915; 1.42.
⎱ Chiclet, Nov. 8, 1916; 1.42.

1 mile 50 yds., Vox Populi, Sept. 5, 1908; 1.40 4/5.

1 mile 55 yds., First Whip, Aug 22, 1900; 1.43¼.

1 mile 60 yds., Watervale, May 9, 1911; 1.42 2/5.

1 mile 70 yds., Pif, Jr., May 29, 1918; 1.41 3/5.

1 mile 100 yds., Rapid Water, Nov. 30, 1907; 1.44 1/5.

1 1/16 mile, Celesta, Sept. 3, 1914; 1.42¾.

1⅛ miles, Goaler, June 10, 1921, 1.49; Grey Lag, July 7, 1921, 1.49.

1 3/16 mile, Sir Barton, Aug. 28, 1920; 1.55 3/5.

1¼ mile, Whisk Broom, II, June 28, 1913; 2.00.

1 mile 500 yds., Swiftwing, July 8, 1905; 2.10 1/5.

1 5/16 miles, Ballot, July 1, 1904; 2.09 3/5.

1⅜ miles, Man o' War, June 12, 1920; 2.14 1/5.

1½ miles, Thunderclap, Oct. 11, 1919; 2.29 3/5.

1⅝ miles, Man o' War, Sept. 4, 1920; 2.40 4/5.

1¾ miles, Maj. Daingerfield, Oct. 3, 1903; 2.57.

1⅞ miles, Orcagna, March 2, 1909; 3.17 3/5.

2 miles, Everett, Oct. 31, 1910; 3.25 3/5.

2 miles 70 yards., Grosgrain, Jan. 27, 1906; 3.35 1/5.

2 1/16 miles, War Whoop, Sept. 23, 1905; 3.34¼.

2⅛ miles, Joe Murphy, Aug. 30, 1894; 3.42.

2¼ miles, Ethelbert, Aug. 4, 1900; 3.49 1/5.

2½ miles, Kyrat, Nov. 18, 1899; 4.24½.

2⅝ miles, Ten Broeck, Sept. 16, 1876; 4.58½.

2¾ miles, Hubbard, Aug. 9, 1873; 4.58¾.

3 miles, Mamie Algol, Feb. 16, 1907; 5.19.

4 miles ⎰ Lucret. Borgia, May 20, 1897; 7.11.
⎱ Sotemia, Oct. 7, 1912; 7.10 1/5.

WORLD'S RECORDS RUNNING HORSES—HALF MILE TRACK

¼ mile—Sam F., June 18, 1909; .23.

½ mile—Booger Red, June 18, 1909; .48½.

⅝ mile—Sepulveda, Sept. 19, 1912; 1.01.

WORLD'S RECORDS RUNNING HORSES OVER HURDLES

1 mile, 4 hurdles, Bob Thomas, Aug. 13, 1890; 1.49.

2 miles, Charawind, Oct. 6, 1903; 3.41 3/5.

3 miles, Alert Dream, March 3, 1909; 5.47¾.

2 miles, steeplechase, Findowrie, Dec. 27, 1909; 3.52¼.

3 miles, steeplechase, Fincastle, Sept. 30, 1911; 5.55¾.

3 miles, 1 furlong, steeplechase, Iolaus, July 10, 1920; 6.15¾.

4 miles, steeplechase, Cuffs, Aug. 10, 1918; 7.49½.

RECORDS OF FAMOUS RUNNING RACES

Saratoga Handicap

Fastest Time—x 1901, Rockton (116); Time, 1.53 1/5.

* 1920, Sir Barton (129); Time, 2.01 4/5.

Slowest Time—* Olambala (128); Time, 2.08 3/5.

x Distance 1⅛ miles; * Distance 1¼ miles.

Brooklyn Handicap

Fastest Time—x 1917 Borrow (117); Time, 1.49 2/5.

Slowest Time—* 1895 Hornpipe (105); Time, 2.11¼.

x Distance 1⅛ miles; * Distance 1¼ miles.

Latonia Derby

Fastest Time—1911, Gov. Gray (124).

1914, John Gun (122); Time, 2.30 2/5.

Slowest Time—1894, Lazzarone (117); Time, 2.51.

Suburban Handicap

Fastest Time—1913, Whisk Broom II (139); Time, 2.00.

Slowest Time—1886, Troubadour (115); Time, 2.12¼.

Saratoga Cup

Fastest Time—x 1901, Blues, (113); Time, 2.52 2/5.

Slowest Time—* 1886, Voante (118); Time, 4.25.

x Distance, 1⅝ miles; * Distance, 2¼ miles.

WORLD'S RECORD TROTTING HORSES

¼ Mile—Uhlan, Oct. 6, 1913; .27.

½ Mile—Lou Dillon, Sept. 17, 1904; .58¾.

¾ Mile—Lou Dillon, Oct. 24, 1903; 1.28½.

1 mile, Peter Manning (5 yrs. old), Oct. 6, 1921, 1.57 3/5.

1 mile, in a race, Hamburg Belle, Aug. 25, 1909; 2.01¼.

1 mile, ½ mile track, Uhlan, Aug. 24, 1911; 2.02¾.

1 mile, Stallion, Lee Axworthy, Oct. 8, 1916; 1.58¼.

1 mile, Gelding, Uhlan, Oct. 8, 1912; 1.58.

1 mile, Peter Manning, Sept., 1921, 1.58.

1 mile, mare, Lou Dillon, Oct. 24, 1903; 1.58½.

1 mile, with running mate, Uhlan, Oct. 9, 1913; 1.54½.

1 mile, yearling, Airdale, Oct. 2, 1912; 2.15¾.

1 mile, two-year old, The Real Lady, Oct. 7, 1916; 2.04¼.

1 mile, 3 year old, Sister Bertha, Oct. 12, 1920; 2.02¾.

1 mile, 3 year old Gelding, Czar Worthy, Sept. 16, 1921; 2.03¾.

1 mile, by 4 year old, Arion Guy, Oct. 6, 1921; 1.59½.

1 mile, 5 year old, Lee Axworthy, Oct. 8, 1916; 1.58¼.

1 mile, six year old, Lou Dillon, Nov. 11, 1904; 2.01.

1 mile, high-wheel sulky, Peter Billiken, Aug. 20, 1914; 2.14¼.

1 mile, high wheel sulky, Major Delmar, Oct. 26, 1904; 2.07.

Best two heats, Hamburg Belle, Aug. 25, 1909; 2.01¼, 2.01¾.

Best 3 heats, Peter Manning, Oct. 7, 1920; 2.03, 2.02¾, 2.02½.

2 miles, The Harvester, Oct. 13, 1910; 4.15¼.

3 miles, Nightingale, Oct. 20, 1893; 6.55½.
　　　　　　Fairy Wood, July 1, 1895; 7.16½.

4 miles, Bertie R., Sept. 11, 1899; 9.58.
　　　　　　Senator L., Nov. 2, 1894; 10.12.

5 miles, Imogene Constantine, Sept. 29, 1919; 12.08¼.

10 miles,　　Pascal, Nov. 2, 1893; 26.15.
　　　　　　Controller, Nov. 23, 1878; 27.23¼.

20 miles, Capt. McGowan, Oct. 31, 1865; 58.25.

30 miles, Gen. Taylor, Feb. 21, 1857; 1.47.59.

50 miles, Ariel, May 5, 1846; 3.55.40½.

100 miles, Conqueror, Nov. 12, 1853; 8.55.53.

WORLD'S RECORD TROTTING—
WAGON

¼ mile, Uhlan, Aug. 11, 1911; 27¾. Last quarter of ½ mile with runner.

½ mile, Uhlan, Aug. 11, 1911; 56¼. Assisted by runner at side.

½ mile, Major Delmar, Gelding, 1.00 (C. K. G. Billings, Amateur, July 31, 1906; 1.00).

1 mile, Lou Dillon, Oct. 23, 1903; 2.00.

With two runners, Uhlan, Aug. 9, 1911, 2.00.

1 mile, Uhlan, Gelding (without wind shield), Aug. 8, 1910; 2.01.

1 mile, Stallion, Lee Axworthy, Aug. 12, 1916; ?.02¾.

1 mile, Lord Derby, 1902; 2.05¾.

1⅛ mile, The Monk, 1902; 2.25½.

2 miles, Dexter, 1865; 4.56¼.

2 miles, Pelagon, Oct. 20, 1909; 4.38.

3 miles, Prince, 1857; 7.53½.

5 miles, Fillmour, 1863; 13.16.

5 miles, Ed Brien, Oct. 30, 1907; 13.03.

10 miles, Julia Aldrich, 1858; 29.04½.

20 miles, Controller, 1878; 58.57.

WORLD'S RECORD TROTTING—
TEAMS
1 mile,
>   Louis Forrest,
>   Uhlan, Oct. 11, 1912; 2.03¼.

1 mile in a race,

> Roy Miller,
> Lucy Van, Sept. 11, 1918;
> 2.10¼.

1 mile, road wagon,

> Maud S.,
> Aldine, June 15, 1883;
> 2.15½.

Best 3 heats in a race,

> Arab,
> Conde, Nov. 26, 1887;
> · 2.29¼; 2.23, 2.18¼.

WORLD'S RECORD TROTTING WITH RUNNING MATE

1 mile against time, Uhlan and mate, Oct. 9, 1913; 1.54½.

1 mile in race, Frank and mate, Nov. 15, 1883; 2.08½.

WORLD'S RECORD TROTTING— HALF MILE TRACK

1 mile, Uhlan, Gelding, Aug. 24, 1911; 2.02¾.

1 mile, Stallion, Harry J. S., Sept. 7, 1917; 2.07½.

1 mile in a race, Axtien, July 4, 1917; 2.09¼.

1 mile, mare, Sweet Marie, Sept. 20, 1907; 2.07.

Fastest 3 heats, Joe Bowers, July 29, 1911; 2.10¾, 2.10¼, 2.10¼.

1 mile 2 wagons, Sweet Marie, Sept. 20, 1907; 2.08½.

2 year old colt, Suldine, Sept. 16, 1915; 2.13¼.

2 year old, Nowaday Girl, Aug. 13, 1912; 2.16¼.

Fastest yearling colt, Verbene Ansel, Sept. 16, 1915; 2.26.

1 mile by team, York Boy and Bemay, Oct. 31, 1902; 2.12¼.

2 miles, Masconoma, Sept. 8, 1906; Exhibition, 4.46.

3 year old stallion, 1 mile, Al Stanley, Aug. 24, 1909; 2.13¼.

3 year old, Hugh Miller, Sept. 18, 1914; 2.11¾.

3 year old colt, Peter Wood, Sept. 2, 1908; 2.19¼.

3 year old, Ripy, Aug. 6, 1908; 2.19¼.

Teams

1 mile (Amateur driver), Ross B. and Brighton B., Sept. 25, 1915; 2.06½.

1 mile (in a race), Roxmiller and Lucy Van, Sept. 11, 1918; 2.10¼.

1 mile (team of mares), Aerolite and Leola, Aug. 26, 1905; 2.10.

WORLD'S RECORD TROTTING HORSES

Trotting Tandem Team

1 mile, Brother Jack and Tom Mountain (on half mile track). Sept., 1910; 2.40.

1 mile, Manbrino Sparkle and William H., 1886; 2.32.

Trotting Team Three Abreast

1 mile, Belle Hamlin, Globe and Justina, 1891; 2.14.

Trotting Team Four in Hand

1 mile, Daminana, Bellnut, Maud V. and Nut-spara; 2.30.

Trotting to High Sulky

1 mile, Major Delmar (same kind of sulky, non-ball bearing; weight 54½ pounds, as used by Maud S.), Oct. 26, 1904; 2.07.

1 mile, Lou Dillon, Sept. 12, 1903; 2.05.

(Maud S.'s famous record was 2.08¾.)

Trotting—Under Saddle

⅛ mile, Uhlan, 1914; .13½.

1 mile, Great Eastern, 1877; 2.15¾.

1 mile, Country Jane, Sept. 15, 1909; 2.08¼.

1 mile, in a race, The Wanderer, 1914; 2.14½.

2 miles, George H. Patchen, 14 years old, 1863; 4.56.

3 miles, Dutchman, 11 years old, 1839; 7.32½.

4 miles, Dutchman, 8 years old, Gelding, 1836; 10.51.

Trotting—Straightaway

¼ mile, Lou Dillon, Nov. 11, 1903; .27.

½ mile, Lou Dillon, Nov. 11, 1903; .59.

Double-Gaited Horse—One Mile

1 mile trotting, Anaconda, Aug. 23, 1904; 2.09¾.

1 mile pacing, Anaconda, Aug. 23, 1904; 2.01¾.

World's Record Trotting—On Ice

¼ mile, Dean Oakley, Feb. 15, 1912; .30½.

½ mile, Bay Seth, Jan. 28, 1911; 1.01.

1 mile, Surena, Sept. 1, 1906; 2.18.

WORLD'S TROTTING CHAMPIONS OF 100 YEARS

Fastest Trotting from 1806 *to the Present Time*

Yankee, 1806; 2.50.

Boston Horse, 1810; 2.48½.

Trouble, 1826; 2.43½.

Sally Miller, 1834; 2.37.

Edwin Forrest, 1838; 2.36½.

Confidence, 1838; 2.36.

Dutchman, 1839; 2.32.

Lady Suffolk, Oct. 13, 1845; 2.29½.

Claim has been made that correct time for Lady Suffolk was 2.26.

Pelham, July 2, 1849; 2.28.

Highland Maid, June 5, 1853; 2.27.

Flora Temple, Sept. 2, 1856; 2.24½.

Flora Temple, Oct. 7, 1859; 2.21½.

Dexter, Aug. 14, 1867; 2.17¼.

Goldsmith Maid, Sept. 6, 1871; 2.17.

Goldsmith Maid, June 9, 1872; 2.16¾.

Occident, Sept. 17, 1873; 2.16¾.

Goldsmith Maid, July 16, 1874; 2.16.

Goldsmith Maid, Sept. 2, 1874; 2.14.

Rarus, Aug. 3, 1878; 2.13¾.

St. Julien, Oct. 25, 1879; 2.12¾.

Maud S., Aug. 12, 1880; 2.11¾.

St. Julien, Aug. 12, 1880; 2.11¾.

Maud S., Sept. 11, 1880; 2.10¾.

Maud S., Aug. 11, 1881; 2.10¼.

Jay Eye See, Aug. 1, 1884; 2.10.

Maud S., Aug. 1, 1884; 2.09.

Maud S., July 30, 1885; 2.08¾.

Sunol, Oct. 20, 1891; 2.08¾.

Nancy Hanks, Sept. 23, 1892; 2.04.

Alix, Sept. 18, 1894; 2.03¾.

Abbot, Sept. 16, 1900; 2.03¾.

Cresceus, Aug. 1, 1901; 2.02¼.

Lou Dillon, Oct. 24, 1903; 1.58½.

Lou Dillon, 1904-1909; 1.58½.

Uhlan, 1910-1911; 1.58¾.

Uhlan, 1912; 1.58.

Uhlan, 1913-1914; 1.54½.

WORLD'S PACING RECORDS

¼ mile, Directum I., Sept. 14, 1916; .26¾ (Paced by two runners).

¼ mile, (to cart with runner) Banboy, Dec. 29, 1912; .30.

½ mile, Directum, Sept. 14, 1916; .55¾. (Paced by two runners).

½ mile, by 2 year old, Dazzle Patch, Sept. 6, 1912; .58½.

¾ mile, Prince Alert, Sept. 23, 1903; 1.26¼.

1 mile, Dan Patch, Sept. 8, 1906; 1.55. (With windshield and pacemaker in front and at his side).

1 mile, Directum I., Sept. 15, 1915; 1.56¾.
(With windshield; aided by pacemaker).

1 mile, against time, Star Pointer, Aug. 28,
1897; 1.59¼ (without windshield).

Capa De Ore, Nov. 8, 1910; 1.59. (Without
windshield).

1 mile, a race, Directum I., Sept. 30, 1914; 1.58.

1 mile, (without windshield or pacemaker),
Audubon Boy, Sept. 22, 1905. 1.59¼.

Dan Patch, Oct. 13, 1905; 1.59¾.

Minor Heir, Nov. 9, 1909; 1.59¼.

1 mile, unpaced, Minor Heir, Sept. 16, 1910;
1.58½.

1 1/16 mile, Directum I., Aug. 16, 1916; 2.09¾.

1⅛ mile, Directum I., Aug. 21, 1916; 2.16¼.

1¼ mile, Nervelo, 1903; 2.38.

1½ miles, Locanda, 1903; 3.15½.

2 miles, Dan Patch, Nov. 30, 1903; 4.17.

3 miles, Joe Jefferson, 12 years old, Nov. 6,
1891; 7.33¼.

4 miles, Joe Jefferson, 12 years old, Nov. 13,
1891; 10.10.

Fastest stallion, Dan Patch, Sept. 8, 1906;
1.55. (With windshield and pacemaker in front
and side).

Fastest gelding, Prince Alert, Sept. 24, 1903;
1.57.

Fastest mare, Miss Harris M., July 23, 1918;
1.58¼.

Fastest mare in race, (1 mile) Evelyn W., Sept.
13, 1912; 2.00½.

Fastest yearling filly, (against time) Rose McGee, Aug. 4, 1914; 2.19½.

Fastest yearling, (1 mile), Frank Perry, Sept. 12, 1911; 2.15.

Fastest yearling gelding, Vice, 1914; 2.23¾.

World's Pacing Records—Teams

1 mile against time, Minor Heir—Geo. Gano, Oct. 1, 1912; 2.02.

1 mile in a race, Billy M. and Doctor M., Sept. 24, 1914; 2.07¼.

1 mile in a race, Cohen and Dep. Sheriff, Aug. 28, 1916; 2.07¼.

World's Records Made by Pacers—To Wagon

¼ mile, Little Indian, Oct. 9, 1907; .34.

½ mile, Dan Patch, Oct. 27, 1903; .56.

½ mile, Morning Star, July 31, 1906; .59½.

1 mile, Dan Patch, Oct. 27, 1903; 1.57¼.

1 mile, Aileen Wilson, Oct. 13, 1910; 2.04½.

1 mile, Angus Pointer, 1904; 2.04½.

1 mile (amateur driver), William, Sept. 16, 1915; 1.59½.

3 miles, Longfellow, 1868; 7.53.

5 miles, Lady St. Clair, 1874; 12.54¾.

World's Record High Wheel Sulky

1 mile, Dan Patch, Nov. 30, 1903; 2.04¾.

World's Record Pacing Under Saddle

½ mile, Symboleer, Sept. 2, 1904; 1.06.

1 mile, George Gano, Sept. 2, 1915; 2.10¼.

1 mile, Billy Boyce, 1868; 2.14¼.

2 miles, Bowery Boy, 1839; 5.04½.

3 miles, Oneida Chief, 1843; 7.44.

World's Record Pacing—Guideless
½ mile, Omas R., Sept. 5, 1911; 1.00½.

World's Record Pacing—Team to Wagon
¼ mile, Prince Direct & Hontas Crook, Sept. 17, 1904; .29¾.

½ mile, Hontas Crook & Prince Direct, Sept. 17, 1904; 1.00¼.

1 mile, Minor Heir & George Gano, Oct. 1, 1912; 2.02.

1 mile (fastest two Heats), Hedgewood Boy & Lady Maude, Sept. 14, 1909; 2.04¼, 2.05¾.

World's Record Pacing—Half Mile Track
½ mile, Billy M., Aug. 4, 1916; 1.00¾.

1 mile, Dan Patch, Sept. 21, 1905; 2.01.

1 mile, Directum I., Aug. 20, 1913; 2.02¾.

1 mile (to wagon), Dan Patch, Sept. 21, 1905; 2.05.

1 mile (Gelding), Roan Hal, Aug. 24, .1917; 2.03¼.

1 mile (Stallion), George Gano, Sept. 22, 1911; 2.04½.

1 mile (filly), Lucille Spiers, July 4, 1916; 2.03¼.

1 mile (Mare), Alcyfras, Aug. 18, 1911; 2.04½.

· 1 mile, John R. Gentry & Prince Albert, 1901 and 1900; 2.04¾.

1 mile, Baron Durham, Oct. 23, 1915; 2.16¾.

1 mile, William, Aug. 27, 1913; 2.09.

1 mile, Franklin Pierce & Buck Muscovite, Aug. 29, 1914; 2.10¼.

3 miles, Elastic Pointer, Sept. 30, 1909; 7.31½.

5 miles, Marconi, Sept. 1, 1917; 12.02¾.

World's Record Pacing—Third-Mile Track

1 mile (Gelding), Mimie, Sept. 1, 1909; 2.09¼.

World's Record by Woman Driver

1 mile, Cord Axworthy, July 20, 1916; 2.18.

WORLD'S RECORD LONG DISTANCE RIDING

10 miles, Madam Maranette Lasing (changing horses), June 2, 1883; 18.17.

50 miles, Carl Pugh (ten horses), July 7, 1883; 1.50.03½.

100 miles, George Osbaldiston, Nov. 5, 1831; 4.19.40.

200 miles, Neil H. Mowry (30 horses), Aug. 2, 1868; 8 hrs.

300 miles, Neil H. Mowry (changing), Aug. 2, 1868; 14 hrs. 9 min.

559 miles & 754 yds., Pinafore against other horses and men in a six day race, Oct. 15 to 20; 1879.

1,071½ miles, C. M. Anderson, April 15-20, 1884; 72 hrs. San Francisco (changing horses at will), 12 hrs. daily.

WORLD'S RECORD HIGH JUMP HORSES

7 ft. 8½ in. (91-92 in.), Biskra (American horse), Aug. 12, 1912; and Mount Joie III (French).

WORLD'S PACING CHAMPIONS

1 mile, Drover, 1839; 2.28.

1 mile, Fanny Ellsler, 1844; 2.27½.

1 mile, Unknown, 1845; 2.23.

1 mile, Pet, 1851; 2.21.

1 mile, Pet, 1852; 2.18½.

1 mile, Pocahontas, 1855; 2.17¼.

1 mile, Sweetzer, 1878; 2.15.

1 mile, Sleepy George, 1879; 2.15½.

1 mile, Sleepy Tom, 1879; 2.14¼.

1 mile, Billy Corbeau, 1879; 2.14¼.

1 mile, Little Brown Jug, 1881; 2.11½.

1 mile, Johnston, 1883; 2.10.

1 mile, Johnston, 1884; 2.06¼.

1 mile, Direct, 1891; 2.06.

1 mile, Hal Pointer, 1892; 2.05¼.

1 mile, Mascot, 1892; 2.04.

1 mile, Flying Jib, 1893; 2.04.

1 mile, Robert J., 1894; 2.01½.

1 mile, John R. Gentry, 1896, 2 hrs. ½ sec.

1 mile, Star Pointer, 1897; 1.59¼.

1 mile, Dan Patch, 1902; 1.59¼.

1 mile, Dan Patch, 1903; 1.56¼.

1 mile, Dan Patch, 1904; 1.56.

1 mile, Dan Patch, 1905; 1.55¼.

1 mile, Dan Patch, 1906-15; 1.55.

WORLD'S RUNNING RECORDS
—AMATEUR

20 yards, .02 4/5, E. B. Bloss, Roxbury, Mass., Feb. 22, 1892.

25 yards, .03, T. Connolly, Boston, Mass., Feb. 27, 1907.

35 yards, .04, A. Duffy, Baltimore, Md., March 29, 1903.

40 yards, .04 1/5, D. Thorney, Madison, Wis., March 23, 1912.

50 yards, .05, H. Allen, Pueblo, Colo., April 16, 1915.

60 yards, .06 2/5, A. F. Duffy, Australia, 1905.

75 yards, .07 1/5, A. F. Duffy, Baltimore, Md., May 2, 1903.

78 yards, .07 4/5, B. J. Wefers, Oak Island, Mass., Aug 1, 1896.

90 yards, .08 4/5, Chas. Paddock, Redlands, March 26, 1921.

100 yards, .09 3/5, Dan. J. Kelly, Spokane, Wash., June 23, 1906.

100 yards, .09 3/5, H. P. Drew, Berkeley, Cal., March 28, 1914.

100 yards, .09 3/5, Chas. Paddock, Berkeley, Cal., March 26, 1921.

Paddock made above record 4 times during 1921.

100 yards, .09 3/5, B. J. Wefers, New York City, May 29, 1896.

100 yards, .09 3/5, A. F. Duffy, New Yor'
May 31, 1902.

100 yards, .09 3/5 C. H. Patchen, London,
June 22, 1912.

100 yards, .09 3/5, A. L. Robinson, Philau
phia, Pa., May 2, 1913.

Indoors

100 yards, .09 2/5, A. T. Meyer, Buffalo, N. Y.,
April 18, 1914.

Special

100 yards, .09 2/5, Minoru Fugii, Tokio, Japan,
on the grass, sworn to by officials of Tokio University, Nov. 14, 1902.

---

105 yards, .10 2/5, H. N. Hargrave, New York
City, Sept. 25, 1901.

109 yards, .11, B. J. Wefers, Lowell, Mass.,
Aug. 29, 1896.

110 yards, .10 1/5, Chas. Paddock, Redlands,
March 26, 1921.

130 yards, .12 2/5, Chas. Paddock, Beverley, Cal.,
March 26, 1921.

150 yards, .14 1/5, Chas. Paddock, Redlands,
March 26, 1921.

200 yards, .19, Chas. Paddock, Redlands, March
26, 1921.

220 yards, .20 4/5, Chas. Paddock, Berkeley,
Cal., March 26, 1921.

300 yards, .30 1/5, Chas. Paddock, Berkeley,
Cal., April 23, 1921.

330 yards, .35, L. E. Meyers, New York City,
Oct. 22, 1881.

yards, .47, M. W. Long, Guttenberg, N. J., , 1900. (Straightaway.)

yards, .47 2/5, J. E. Meredith (Turn) bridge, Mass., May 27, 1916.

ь00 yards, 1.10 4/5, M. W. Sheppard, New ork, Aug. 14, 1910.

880 yards, 1.52½, J. E. Meredith, Philadelphia, Pa., May 13, 1916.

1000 yards, 2.12 1/5, Larry Brown, Philadelphia, Pa., June 11, 1921.

1320 yards, 3.02 4/5, T. P. Conneff, New York City, Aug. 21, 1896.

1 mile, 4.12 3/5, N. S. Taber, July 16, 1915.

2 miles, 9.09 3/5, A. Shrubb, June 11, 1904.

3 miles, 14.17 3/5, A. Shrubb, May 21, 1903.

4 miles, 19.23 2/5, A. Shrubb, June 13, 1904.

5 miles, 24.33 2/5, A. Shrubb, May 12, 1904.

6 miles, 29.59 2/5, A. Shrubb, Nov. 5, 1904.

7 miles, 35.04 3/5, A. Shrubb, Nov. 5, 1904.

8 miles, 40.16, A. Shrubb, Nov. 5, 1904.

9 miles, 45.27 3/5, A. Shrubb, Nov. 5, 1904.

10 miles, 50.40 3/5, A. Shrubb, Nov. 5, 1904.

15 miles, 1 hr. 20.04 2/5, F. Appleby, July 21, 1902.

20 miles, 1 hr. 51.54, G. Grossland, Sept. 22, 1894.

25 miles, 2 hrs. 29.29 2/5, H. Green, May 12, 1913.

One hour, 11 miles, 1442 yds., J. Bouin, July 6, 1913.

Two hours, 20 miles, 952 yds., H. Green, May 12, 1913.

WORLD'S RECORD MARATHON RACE
26 miles—385 yards

2 hrs. 36 mins. 26 1/5 secs., Matthew Maloney, Rye, N. Y., to Columbus Circle), Dec. 26, 1908.

Professional

2 hrs. 44 mins. 20 2/5 secs., Dorondo Pietrie, Mad. Square Garden, N. Y., Nov. 25, 1908.

WORLD'S RUNNING RECORDS— METRIC

100 meters, .10 2/5, Chas. Paddock, April 25, 921.

200 meters, .21 1/5, Chas. Paddock, April 23, 921.

300 meters, .33 1/5, Chas. Paddock, April 23, 921.

400 meters, .48 1/5, C. Reidpath, 1912.

500 meters, 1.05 6/10, H. D. Mountain, Sept. 1, 1921.

800 meters, 1.51.9, J. E. Meredith, 1912.

1000 meters, 2.32.3, Mickler, 1913.

1500 meters, 3.55.8, A. R. Kiviat, 1912.

3000 meters, 8.36.8, H. Kolehmainen, 1912.

5000 meters, 14.36.6, H. Kolehmainen, 1912.

10,000 meters, 30.58.8, J. Bouin, 1913.

10,000 meters, 31.20.8, H. Kolehmainen, 1912.

15 kilometers, 47.18.6, J. Bouin, 1913.

20 kilometers, 1h. 7m. 57.4s., A. Ahlgren, 1913.

One hour, 19,021m., 90cm., J. Bouin, 1913.

WORLD'S RUNNING RECORDS—
PROFESSIONAL

50 yards, .05¼, H. M. Johnson, New York, Nov. 22, 1884.

75 yards, .07 1/5, A. B. Postal, Auckland, New Zealand, Aug. 16, 1912.

100 yards, .09 3/5, E. S. Donovan, Brockton, Mass., Sept. 2, 1895.

100 yards, .09 3/5, Geo. Seward (Flying Start), Hammersmith, Eng., Sept. 30, 1844.

120 yards, .11, Jack Donaldson, Pretoria, S. A., Nov. 13, 1909.

130 yards, .12, A. B. Postal, Menzies, Australia, April 16, 1906.

130 yards, .12, J. Donaldson, Scotland, July 26, 1913.

140 yards, .13, A. B. Postal, Kalgoorlie, Aus., March 14, 1907.

150 yards, .14, J. Donaldson, Kimberley, S. A., January 21, 1911.

200 yards, .19½, G. Seward, Parkes, Eng., March 22, 1847.

300 yards, .29¾, J. Donaldson, Manchester, Eng., Aug. 4, 1913.

440 yards, .47 4/5, R. B. Day, Perth, West Australia, April 1, 1907.

600 yards, 1.13, E. C. Bredin, England, July 31, 1897.

880 yards, 1.53½, F. S. Hewitt, Littleton, New Zealand, Sept. 21, 1871.

¾ mile, 3.07, W. Richards, England, June 30, 1866.

1 mile, 4.12¾, W. G. George, England, Aug.
23, 1866.

2 miles, 9.12½, W. Lang, Manchester, England,
Aug. 1, 1863.

3 miles, 14.19½, P. Cannon, Scotland, May 14,
1888.

4 miles, 19.25 3/5, P. Cannon, Scotland, Nov. 8,
888.

5 miles, 24.40, J. White, Hackney Wicks, Lon-
lon, May 11, 1863.

10 miles, 50.55, Geo. McCrane, England, 1918.

Six days go as you please, 4 hours a day, 24
lours, 195 miles, George D. Noremac, Aberdeen,
Scotland, week June 5, 1889.

72-hour races, 12 hours daily. Greatest distance
raveled, go-as-you-please, 6-day race; England,
130 miles. C. Rowell, London, April 27 to May 2,
885. American record, 415 miles 125 yds., G.
D. Noremac, Easton, Pa., March 14-19, 1887.

142 hours, go-as-you-please. George Littlewood,
England, 623 miles; James Alberts, U. S. A.,
121 miles; P. Fitzgerald, 610 miles; Chas. Rowell,
02 miles; George Noremac, 566 miles; Frank
Hart, 565 miles; E. P. Weston, 550 miles; H. O.
Messler, 526 miles; Peter Hegelman, 526 miles.

WORLD'S WALKING RECORDS— AMATEUR

75 yards, .11 4/5, W. H. Fitzpatrick, New Or-
eans, La., May 15, 1911.

⅛ mile, .36 3/5, Wm. Young, Portland, Ore.,
Aug. 3, 1905.

¼ mile, 1.22 1/5, F. H. Kramer, Auckland, N. Z., March 20, 1897.

½ mile, 3.00, F. H. Kramer, Auckland, N. Z., March 20, 1897.

¾ mile, 4.40½, T. H. Armstrong, New York City, Oct. 26, 1877.

1⅛ miles, 6.39 1/5, Wm. Plant, Brooklyn, N. Y., March 31, 1920.

1 mile, 6.25 4/5, G. H. Goulding, Canada, June 4, 1910.

1¼ miles, 8.20 4/5, G. H. Goulding, Brooklyn, N. Y., March 30, 1912.

1½ miles, 10.06, G. H. Goulding, Brooklyn, N. Y., March 30, 1912.

1¾ miles, 11.42 1/5, G. H. Goulding, Brooklyn, N. Y., March 30, 1912.

2 miles, 13.11 2/5, G. E. Larner, England, July 13, 1904.

2¼ miles, 15.25 2/5, G. H. Goulding, Brooklyn, N. Y., March 30, 1912.

2½ miles, 17.13 1/5, G. H. Goulding, Brooklyn, N. Y., March 30, 1912.

2¾ miles, 19.00 4/5, G. H. Goulding, Brooklyn, N. Y., March 30, 1912.

3 miles, 20.25 4/5, G. E. Larner, England, Aug. 19, 1905.

3¼ miles, 22.36 3/5, G. H. Goulding, Brooklyn, N. Y., March 30, 1912.

3½ miles, 24.26 3/5, G. H. Goulding, Brooklyn, N. Y., March 30, 1912.

3¾ miles, 26.17 3/5, G. H. Goulding, Brooklyn, N. Y., March 30, 1912.

4 miles, 27.14, G. E. Larner, England, Aug. 19, 1905.

4¼ miles, 32.27¼, W. H. Purdy, Greenpoint, L. I., Aug. 9, 1879.

4½ miles, 34.23¾, W. H. Purdy, Greenpoint, L. I., Aug. 9, 1879.

4¾ miles, 36.21¾, W. H. Purdy, Greenpoint, L. I., Aug. 9, 1879.

5 miles, 36.00 1/5, G. E. Larner, England, Sept. 30, 1905.

6 miles, 43.26 1/5, G. E. Larner, England, Sept. 30, 1905.

7 miles, 50.40 4/5, G. H. Goulding, New Brunswick, N. J., Oct. 23, 1915.

8 miles, 58.18 2/5, G. E. Larner, London, Eng., Sept. 30, 1905.

9 miles, 1.7.37 4/5, G. E. Larner, Stadium, London, England, July 17, 1908.

10 miles, 1.15.57 2/5, G. E. Larner, London, England, July 17, 1908.

11 miles, 1.24.09 4/5, Robert Bridge, Stamford Bridge, England, May 2, 1914.

15 miles, 1.56.26, Robert Bridge, Stamford Bridge, England, May 2, 1914.

20 miles, 2.49.26, H. V. L. Ross, London, England, J. Butler, London, June 12, 1913.

25 miles, 3.37.06 3/5, S. C. A. Schofield, Herne Hill, England, May 20, 1911.

22 miles, 3.09.48 4/5, S. C. A. Schofield, Herne Hill, England, May 20, 1911.

50 miles, 7.52.27, J. Butler, Velodrome, London, England, July 12, 1905.

75 miles, 13.11.44, T. E. Hammond, London, England, Sept. 12, 1908.

100 miles, 18.04.10 1/5, T. E. Hammond, London, England, Sept. 12, 1908.

By Hours

1 hour, 8 miles, 438 yards, G. E. Larner, London, England, Sept. 30, 1905.

2 hours, 15 miles 128 yards, H. V. L. Ross, England, May 20, 1911.

3 hours, 21 miles 347½ yards, H. V. L. Ross, London, England, June 12, 1913.

10 hours, 61 miles 1237 yards, E. C. Horton, Stamford Bridge, England, May 2, 1914.

12 hours, 73 miles 145 yards, E. C. Horton, Stamford Bridge, England, May 2, 1914.

15 hours, 84 miles 574 yards, W. Brown, London, England, Sept. 17, 1909.

24 hours, 131 miles 580 yards, T. E. Hammond, London, England, Sept. 11-12, 1908.

24 hours (without stop), 127 miles 542 yards, T. Payne, London, England, Sept. 18, 1909 (3 laps to mile).

WORLD'S WALKING RECORDS—PROFESSIONAL

1 mile, 6.22, Geo. Cummins, Manchester, England, Aug. 4, 1913.

2 miles, 13.14, J. W. Raby, Lillie Bridge, England, Aug. 20, 1883.

3 miles, 20.21½, J. W. Raby, Lillie Bridge, England, Aug. 20, 1883.

4 miles, 27.38, J. W. Raby, Lillie Bridge, England, Aug. 20, 1883.

5 miles, 35.10, J. W. Raby, Lillie Bridge, England, Aug. 20, 1883.

6 miles, 43.01, J. W. Raby, Lillie Bridge, England, Aug. 20, 1883.

7 miles, 51.04, J. W. Raby, Lillie Bridge, England, Aug. 20, 1883.

8 miles, 58.44, Jack Hibbard, Lillie Bridge, England, Aug. 20, 1883.

9 miles, 1.07.14, J. W. Raby, Lillie Bridge, England, Aug. 20, 1883.

10 miles, 1.14.45, J. W. Raby, Lillie Bridge, England, Dec. 3, 1883.

15 miles, 1.55.56, J. W. Raby, Lillie Bridge, England, Dec. 3, 1883.

20 miles, 2.39.57, W. Perkins, Lillie Bridge, England, July 16, 1877.

25 miles, 3.35.14, W. Franks, Lillie Bridge, England, Aug. 28, 1882.

50 miles, 7.54.16, J. Hibbard, London, England, May 14, 1888.

100 miles, 18.4, W. A. Hoagland, Auburn, N. Y., Oct. 21-22, 1886.

200 miles, 40.46.30, Geo. Littlewood, Sheffield, England, March 7-11, 1882.

300 miles, 66.30, Geo. Littlewood, Sheffield, England, March 7-11, 1882.

400 miles, 96.51.03, Geo. Littlewood, Sheffield, England, March 7-11, 1882.

500 miles, 130.33.45, Geo. Littlewood, Sheffield, England, March 7-11, 1882.

WORLD'S WALKING RECORDS—PRO-FESSIONAL
(HOURS)

1 hour, 8 miles, 172 yds., W. Griffin, Lillie Bridge, England, Oct. 4, 1881; 8 miles, 302 yds., J. Meagher, New York, Nov. 29, 1882.

2 hours, 15 miles, 824 yds., W. Perkins, Lillie Bridge, England, July 16, 1877; 14 miles, 1320 yds., D. A. Driscoll, New York, Feb. 1, 1887.

3 hours, 22 miles, 456½ yds., H. Thatcher, Lillie Bridge, England, Feb. 20, 1882.

4 hours, 27 miles, 410 yds., W. Franks, Lillie Bridge, England, Aug. 28, 1882; 24 miles, 1152 yds., J. B. Clark, New York, Dec. 5, 1879.

5 hours, 32 miles, 800 yds., W. Hawes, London, England, March 30, 1878.

6 hours, 38 miles, 750 yds., W. Hawes, London, England, March 30, 1878.

7 hours, 44 miles, 500 yds., W. Hawes, London, England, March 30, 1878.

8 hours, 50 miles, 1010 yds., J. Hibbard, London, England, May 14, 1888.

9 hours, 56 miles, 300 yds., J. Hibbard, London, England, May 14, 1888.

10 hours, 61 miles, 1200 yds., J. Hibbard, London, England, May 14, 1888.

11 hours, 66 miles, 1300 yds., J. Hibbard, London, England, May 14, 1888.

12 hours, 70 miles, 677 yds., J. Hibbard, Sheffield, England, May 14, 1888.

24 hours, 127 miles, 1219 yds., W. Hawes, London, England, Feb. 23, 1878.

48 hours, 219 miles, 812 yds., G. Littlewood, Sheffield, England, March 6, 1882.

72 hours, 308 miles, 1083 yds., G. Littlewood, Sheffield, England, March 7-11, 1882.

96 hours, 396 miles, 271 yds., G. Littlewood, Sheffield, England, March 7-11, 1882.

120 hours, 470 miles, 1354 yds., G. Littlewood, Sheffield, England, March 7-11, 1882.

144 hours, 531 miles, 135 yds., G. Littlewood, Sheffield, England, March 7-11, 1882. Actual walking time, 138 hours 48 min. 30 sec.

1546 miles, Edward Payson Weston, age 75, New York to Minneapolis, June 2-Aug. 2, 1913.

INDOOR AND OUTDOOR ATHLETICS —AMATEUR

WORLD'S RECORD HOP, STEP AND JUMP

50 feet 11 inches, D. F. Ahearn, Celtic Park, N. Y., May 30, 1911.

WORLD'S RECORD STANDING BROAD JUMP

11 feet 4⅞ inches, R. C. Ewry, St. Louis, Mo., Aug. 24, 1904.

WORLD'S RECORD STANDING HIGH JUMP

5 feet 5¾ inches, L. Goehring, Travers Island, N. Y., June 14, 1913.

WORLD'S RECORD STANDING THREE JUMPS

35 feet 8¾ inches, R. C. Ewry, Celtic Park, N. Y., Sept. 7, 1903.

WORLD'S RECORD POLE VAULT

13 feet 5⅛ inches, F. K. Foss, Olympic Games, Antwerp, August, 1920.

WORLD'S RECORD RUNNING BROAD JUMP

25 feet 3 inches, Ned Gourdin, Cambridge, Mass., July 23, 1921.

WORLD'S RECORDS HURDLING

110 meters, .14 4/5, E. J. Thomson, Antwerp, Belgium, May 28, 1920.

200 meters, .24 3/5, H. L. Hillman, 1904.

400 meters, .54, F. Loomis, Antwerp, Belgium, May, 1920.

120 yards, .15, F. C. Smithson, July 25, 1908.

220 yards, .23 3/5, A. Kraenzien, New York, May 28, 1898.

220 yards, .23 3/5, J. I. Wendell, Boston, May 31, 1913.

220 yards, .23 3/5, R. Simpson, Columbia, Mo., May 27, 1916.

440 yards, .56 4/5, G. R. L. Anderson, July 16, 1910.

WORLD'S RECORD RUNNING HIGH JUMP

6 ft. 7 5/16 in., E. Beeson (old style), Berkeley, Cal., May 2, 1914.

6 ft. 4½ in., R. Landon (new style), Antwerp, Olympic Games, August, 1920.

6 ft. 4¾ in., Clinton Larsen (without weights—indoors), Salt Lake, March 26, 1920.

STANDING HIGH JUMP

5 ft. 5¼ in., Leo Goehring (without weights, outdoors), New York City, June 14, 1913.

5 ft. 4⅛ in., Platt Adams (indoors), New York City, Jan. 25, 1913.

JUMPING RECORDS

One standing broad jump, with weights, 12 ft. 9½ in., L. Hellwig, Nov. 20, 1884.

One standing broad jump, backwards, with weights, 9 ft., J. J. Carpenter, Nov. 8, 1884.

Two standing broad jumps, with weights, 24 ft., J. E. Payne, Feb. 2, 1895.

Two standing broad jumps, indoor, without weights, 22 ft. 1½ in., Ed. Emes, Dec. 12, 1914.

Three standing broad jumps, with weights, 35 ft. 9 in., W. S. Lawton, May 13, 1876.

Nine standing broad jumps, without weights, 100 ft. 4 in., M. W. Ford, June 7, 1885.

Ten standing broad jumps, without weights, 116 ft. 3½ in., Dr. B. F. Mulligan, Sept. 1, 1902.

Standing hop, step and jump, without weights, 30 ft. 3 in., J. Cosgrove, April 25, 1894.

Standing hop, step and jump, with weights, 31 ft. 7 in., W. W. Butler, June 18, 1886.

Standing jump, step and jump, without weights, 32 ft. 4½ in., Platt Adams, Sept. 6, 1909.

Running two hops and jump, without weights, 50 ft. 11 in., D. F. Ahearn, July 31, 1909.

INDOOR AND OUTDOOR ATHLETICS
—PROFESSIONAL

RUNNING HIGH JUMP
6 ft. ½ in., E. W. Johnston, Boston, Mass., Oct. 1, 1881.

RUNNING BROAD JUMP
23 ft. 1 in., L. A. Carpenter, Boston, Mass., Oct. 16, 1896.

HOP, STEP AND JUMP
48 ft. 8 in., T. Burrows, Worcester, Mass., Oct. 18, 1884.

POLE VAULT
11 ft. 9 in., R. B. Dickerson, Ireland, July 11, 1892.

STANDING BROAD JUMP
12 ft. ½ in., J. Darby, England, May 28, 1890.

STANDING HIGH JUMP
4 ft. 11 in., H. Andrews, Scotland, June 28, 1875.

STANDING THREE JUMPS
36 ft. 3 in., T. Colquitt, England, May 5, 1907.

WORLD'S JUMPING RECORDS—PRO-FESSIONAL

Standing high jump, with weights, 6 ft. 5½ in., J. Darby, England, Feb. 5, 1892.

Running high jump, with weights, 6 ft. 7 in., Louis Guertin, Revere, Mass., July 4, 1905.

Running high jump, without weights, 6 ft. 1 in., M. F. Sweeney.

Standing jump for distance, without weights, 12 ft. 1½ in., J. Darby, England, May 28, 1890.

Standing jump for distance, with weights, 14 ft. 9 in., J. Darby; 15 ft. 4 in., R. P. Williams, New London, Conn., 1905.

Standing three jumps, with weights, 42 ft. 2½ in., R. W. Baker, Revere, Mass., July 4, 1905.

Running jump for distance, without weights, 24 ft. 6 in., R. P. Williams, Milford, N. S., July 12, 1905.

Running jump for distance, with weights, 29 ft. 7 in., J. Howard, Chester, England, May 8, 1854.

Running hop, step and jump, without weights, 48 ft. 8 in., T. Burrows, Worcester, Mass.

Standing hop, step and jump, without weights, 10 ft. 5 in., D. Anderson, England, July 24, 1865.

Running two hops and jump, without weights, 49 ft. 6 in., T. Burrows, England, June 3, 1882.

Running high kick, 10 ft., 3 in., R. P. Williams, New London, Conn., 1905.

Running hitch and kick, 9 ft. 6 in., R. P. Williams, New London, Conn., 1905.

Standing two hops and jump, 36 ft. 10 in., Charles Matthews, Salford, England, August, 1905.

Standing hop and jump, 24 ft. 7 in., Charles Matthews, Salford, England, August, 1905.

Standing three jumps, without weights, 41 ft. 10½ in., C. Matthews, Colton, England, Sept. 3, 1904.

Standing three jumps, with weights, 42 ft. 9 in., T. Colquitt, England, May, 1907.

Standing five jumps, without weights, 61 ft. 5½ in., J. Darby, Dumley, England, May 28, 1890.

Standing five jumps, with weights, 76 ft. 3 in., J. Darby, Dumley, England, May 28, 1890.

Standing ten jumps, with weights, 130 ft. 8 in., J. Darby.

Standing back jump, with weights, 12 ft. 11 in., J. Darby, Haden, England, Sept. 14, 1891; R. P. Williams, New London, Conn., Aug. 25, 1910, 13 ft. 3 in.

WORLD'S RECORDS RELAY RACES —AMATEUR
(Outdoors)

440 yds. relay, .42 2/5, 4 men, each man ran 110 yds., B. J. Wefers, Jr., F. K. Lovejoy, H. Ray, Ed. Farrell, Pasadena, Cal., July 5, 1921.

880 yds. relay, 1.27 2/5, 4 men, each man ran 220 yds., B. J. Wefers, Jr., F. K. Lovejoy, H. Ray, Ed. Farrell, Pasadena, Cal., July 5, 1921.

One mile relay, 3.16 2/5, 4 men with baton, each ran 440 yds., C. D. Rogers, Earl Eby, Larry Brown, R. S. Maxam, Philadelpha, Pa. June 11, 1921.

Two-mile relay, 7.50 2/5, 4 men, each ran 880 yds., W. R. Milligan, H. B. Stallard, W. G. Tatham and G. B. D. Rudd, Philadelphia, Pa., May 1, 1921.

One mile, 3.18 1/5 (Schaaf, Gissing, Sheppard, Rosenberger), Sept. 4, 1911.

Two miles, 7.53 (Reiley, Bromilow, Sheppard, Kiviat), Sept. 5, 1910.

Four miles, 17.51 1/5 (Mahoney, Marceau, Powers, Hedlund), June 17, 1913.

400 metres (outdoor, 4 men, each ran 100 metres), .42 1/5 (Murchison, Scholz, Kirksey and Paddock), Olympic Games, 1920.

800 metres (outdoor), 4 men, each man ran 200 metres), 1.27 (Landers, Davis, Haymond, Smith of U. of Penn. team), June 7, 1919.

1600 metres, 3.16 6/10 (Sheppard, Meredith, Reidpath, Lindberg), 1912.

WORLD'S RECORDS—SACK RACING

35 yards, .05 3/5, R. Mercer, March 15, 1901.

40 yards, .06 2/5, F. M. Pearson, Oct. 5, 1905.

50 yards, over 4 hurdles, 1 ft. high, .09¾, J. M. Nason, Dec. 6, 1890.

50 yards, .07, R. Mercer, April 20, 1901.

60 yards, .09, J. M. Nason, April 18, 1891.

65 yards, .09 3/5 J. T. Norton, Jan. 13, 1897.

75 yards, .10 4/5, R. Mercer, April 20, 1901.

75 yards, over 6 hurdles 1 foot high, .16, J. M. Nason, Dec. 6, 1890.

100 yards (indoor), .15, Irving Picard, April 12, 1913.

100 yards, over 10 hurdles 18 in. high, .21¼, J. M. Nason, Sept. 29, 1882.

110 yards, .25 1/5, J. M. Nason, May 12, 1883.

110 yards, over 10 hurdles, each lift 18 in. high, .21, C. M. Cohen, Sept. 19, 1896.

176 yards, .26 4/5, F. A. Onderdonk, April 28, 1903.

One-ninth of a mile, .35 2/5, J. H. Clark, Nov. 22, 1884.

WORLD'S RECORD—RUNNING BACK-WARDS

50 yards, .07 4/5, S. S. Schuyler, Oct. 8, 1887.

75 yards, .11 1/5, S. S. Schuyler, Oct. 8, 1887.

100 yards, .14, A. Forrester, June 23, 1888.

WORLD'S RECORD—HOPPING

50 yards, .07 1/5, S. D. See, Oct. 15, 1885.

80 yards, .10 4/5, S. D. See, Oct. 15, 1885.

100 yards, .13 3/5, S. D. See, Oct. 15, 1885.

WORLD'S RECORD—THREE LEGGED RACES

40 yards, .05 1/5, H. L. Hillman, Jr., and Lawson Robertson, Feb. 20, 1909.

50 yards, .06, H. L. Hillman, Jr., and Lawson Robertson, Nov. 11, 1905.

60 yards, .07 1/5, H. L. Hillman, Jr., and Lawson Robertson, Nov. 11, 1905.

70 yards, .08 2/5, George E. Hall and Lyndon Pierce, April 15, 1908.

75 yards, .08 4/5, H. L. Hillman, Jr., and Lawson Robertson, Feb. 2, 1907.

90 yards (indoor), .10 1/5, W. J. Keating and W. Slade, May 2, 1910.

100 yards, .11, H. L. Hillman, Jr., and Lawson Robertson, April 24, 1900.

110 yards, .12 3/5, H. L. Hillman, Jr., and Lawson Robertson, Nov. 17, 1906.

120 yards, .14, H. L. Hillman, Jr., and Lawson Robertson, Nov. 17, 1906.

150 yards, .20 2/5, C. S. Busse and C. L. Jacquelin, Aug. 31, 1889.

176 yards, .24, C. S. Busse and H. H. Morrell, April 4, 1891.

200 yards, .28½, A. Randolph and H. D. Reynolds, May 24, 1880.

220 yards, .27 1/5, C. Cassasa and S. C. Northridge, Oct. 10, 1909.

1/6 mile, .56, M. A. Dewey and W. J. Battey, Dec. 31, 1879.

1/5 mile, 1.25 2/5, P. Ayers and H. F. McCoy, Nov. 26, 1885.

WORLD'S RECORD VAULTING

Fence vaulting, 7 ft. 3¾ in., C. H. Atkinson, March 22, 1884.

One-hand fence vaulting, 5 ft. 6½ in., I. D. Webster, April 6, 1886.

Bar vaulting, 7 ft. 4 in., T. C. Page, May 8, 1881.

WORLD'S RECORD PULLING BODY UP BY ARMS

Pulling the body up by the little finger of one hand, 6 times, A. Cutter, Sept. 18, 1878.

Pulling the body up by one arm, 12 times, A. Cutter, Sept. 18, 1878.

Pulling the body up by both arms, 65 times, H. H. Seelye, October, 1875.

WORLD'S RECORD IN LIFTING

Lifting with the hands alone, 1,384 lbs., H. Leussing, March 31, 1880.

Lifting with harness, 3,239 lbs., W. B. Curtis, Dec. 20, 1868.

Lifting the bar bell, 246 lbs., Perikles Kakousis, Aug. 31, 1904.

WORLD'S RECORD SHOT PUTTING— AMATEUR

8-lb. shot, 67 ft. 7 in., Ralph Rose, Sept. 14, 1907.

12-lb. shot, 57 ft. 3 in., Ralph Rose, Aug. 29, 1908.

16-lb. shot, 51 ft., Ralph Rose, Aug. 21, 1909.

18-lb. shot (7 ft. circle, outdoor), 46 ft. 2¾ in., P. J. McDonald, May 30, 1914.

18-lb. shot (indoor), 45 ft. 5¾ in., Ralph Rose, Feb. 21, 1913.

24-lb. shot (outdoor), 38 ft. 10 11/16 in., P. J. McDonald, Oct. 22, 1911.

24-lb. shot (indoor, from board to dirt pit), 39 ft. 3¼ in., P. J. McDonald, March 6, 1913.

28-lb. weight with follow (indoor), 36 ft. 8½ in., P. Ryan, Feb. 14, 1914.

28-lb. shot, 34 ft. 5¾ in., Ralph Rose, Sept. 14, 1907.

42-lb. stone, with follow, 28 ft. 11¼ in., P. Ryan, Sept. 1, 1913.

56-lb. shot, with follow, 23 ft. ½ in., W. Real, Oct. 4, 1888.

WORLD'S RECORD WEIGHT THROW-ING—AMATEUR

14-lb. weight thrown from shoulder, with follow, 58 ft. 2 in., J. S. Mitchel, Oct. 4, 1888.

28-lb. weight with follow, 36 ft. 3 in., Dennis Horgan, Sept. 29, 1906.

35-lb. weight for height, 21 ft., P. Ryan, April 12, 1913.

35-lb. weight for distance, 57 ft. ⅞ in., P. Ryan, Sept. 1, 1913.

56-lb. weight thrown from side, with one hand, without run or follow, 28 ft. 9 in., J. S. Mitchel, Aug. 26, 1905.

56-lb. weight, thrown from the side, with two hands, without run or follow, 31 ft. 5 in., John Flanagan, Aug. 26, 1905.

56-lb. weight, thrown with two hands, unlimited run and follow, 43 ft. 1½ in., M. J. McGrath, Oct. 2, 1917.

56-lb. weight, Irish style, one hand, with unlimited run and follow, 38 ft. 5 in., J. S. Mitchel, Sept. 7, 1903.

56-lb. weight, from stand, 33 ft. 1 in., M. J. McGrath, Sept. 24, 1910.

56-lb. weight over bar, 15 ft. 2⅝ in., P. Donovan, Oct. 25, 1913.

56-lb. weight (height), 16 ft. 11¼ in., P. Donovan, Feb. 20, 1914.

WORLD'S RECORD SHOT PUTTING— PROFESSIONAL

Putting 12-lb. shot, 50 ft. ½ in., J. McPherson.

Putting 14-lb. shot, 51 ft. 4 in., C. J. Currie.

Putting 16-lb. shot, 48 ft. 6 in., Robert W. Maxwell, June 15, 1907.

Putting 22-lb. shot, 37 ft. 8 in., C. McLean.

WORLD'S RECORD WEIGHT THROWING—PROFESSIONAL

Throwing 56-lb. weight, 7 ft. circle, 28 ft. 5 in., P. Foley.

Throwing 56-lb. weight, one hand, with unlimited run, 39 ft. 9½ in., Dennis Mahoney, June 4, 1906.

Throwing 12-lb. hammer, without follow, 133 ft. 5½ in., G. Perrie.

Throwing 12-lb. hammer from 7 ft. circle, 184 ft. 6 in., T. Carroll.

Throwing 16-lb. hammer, without follow, 119 ft. ½ in., G. H. Johnstone.

Throwing 16-lb. hammer from 7 ft. circle, 165 ft., T. Carroll.

Throwing 21-lb. hammer without follow, 79 ft., G. Davidson.

Throwing 21-lb. hammer from 7 ft. circle, 112 ft. 1½ in., T. Carroll.

Throwing 21-lb. hammer from 9 ft. circle, 121 ft. 10 in., T. Carroll.

WORLD'S RECORD HAMMER THROWING—AMATEUR

Regulation hammer, A. A. U. rules, weight (including handle) 12 lbs., entire length 4 ft., thrown from 7-ft. circle.

12-lb. hammer, 213 ft. 9⅛ in., P. Ryan, Oct. 19, 1913.

Hammer with handle 3 ft. 6 in. long, thrown with both hands from a mark without run or follow.

12-lb. hammer head, 116 ft. 4 in., C. A. J.)ueckberner, Nov. 17, 1888.

16-lb. hammer head, 100 ft. 5 in., C. A. J.)ueckberner, Nov. 17, 1888. ,

Hammer with handle 4 ft. long, thrown with ne hand from a mark, without run or follow.

8-lb. hammer, 157 ft. 9 in., W. L. Coudon, ιug. 9, 1884.

10-lb. hammer, 140 ft. 2 in., W. L. Coudon, ιug. 9, 1884.

12-lb. hammer head, 119 ft. 1 in., W. L. Coudon, une 25, 1890.

16-lb. hammer, including weight of head and .andle, 101 ft. 5½ in., W. L. Coudon, Aug. 13, 890.

Hammer with handle 4 ft. long, thrown with oth hands from a mark without run or follow.

10-lb. hammer head, 134 ft. 3 in., W. L. Cou-on, May 10, 1888.

12-lb. hammer head, 124 ft. 11 in., W. L. Cou-on, May 10, 1888.

14-lb. hammer head, 115 ft. 4 in., W. L. Cou-lon, May 10, 1888.

16-lb. hammer head, 113 ft. 11 in., W. O. Iickok, May 12, 1894.

Hammer, with handle 4 ft. long, thrown with ne hand, with 7-ft. run and no follow.

8-lb. hammer, including weight of head and ιandle, 210 ft. 3 in., W. L. Coudon, Nov. 5, 1892.

8-lb. hammer head, 180 ft. 7 in., W. L. Cou-lon, Oct. 11, 1889.

12-lb. hammer head, 164 ft. 2 in., W. L. Coudon, Nov. 5, 1882.

16-lb. hammer, including weight of head and handle, 146 ft., E. E. Parry, Aug. 5, 1905.

16-lb. hammer head, 130 ft., J. S. Mitchel, Nov. 6, 1888.

Hammer, with handle 4 ft. long, thrown with both hands, 9-ft. circle.

16-lb. hammer, 189 ft. 3 in., P. Ryan, Sept. 1, 1913.

Hammer, with handle 4 ft. long, thrown with one hand, with unlimited run, but no follow.

8-lb. hammer head, 189 ft. ¼ in., W. L. Coudon, Oct. 11, 1889.

10-lb. hammer, 167 ft. 2 in., W. L. Coudon, Aug. 9, 1894.

Hammer, with handle 4 ft. long, thrown with one hand, with unlimited run and follow.

16-lb. hammer, including weight of head and handle, 129 ft. 11 in., W. L. Coudon, Oct. 8, 1892.

Hammer, with handle 4 ft. long, thrown with both hands, with unlimited run and follow.

16-lb. hammer head, 125 ft. 10 in., J. S. Mitchel, Oct. 1, 1888.

16-lb. hammer, with unlimited run and follow, 180 ft. 1 in., J. J. Flanagan, Oct. 10, 1909.

WORLD'S RECORD HAMMER THROW-ING—PROFESSIONAL

10-lb. hammer, 4 ft. handle, 7 ft. circle, one hand, two turns, 190 ft. 4 in., James McCook, May 4, 1910.

Throwing 12-lb. hammer, without follow, 133
t. 5½ in., G. Perrie.

Throwing 12-lb. hammer from 7-ft. circle, 183
t. 6 in., T. Carroll.

Throwing 16-lb. hammer, without follow, 119 ft.
½ in., G. H. Johnstone.

Throwing 16-lb. hammer from 7-ft. circle, 165
t., T. Carroll.

Throwing 21-lb. hammer, without follow, 79 ft.,
³. Davidson.

Throwing 21-lb. hammer from 7-ft. circle, 112
t. 1½ in., T. Carroll.

Throwing 21-lb. hammer from 9-ft. circle, 121
t. 10 in., T. Carroll.

WORLD'S RECORD DISCUS THROW-ING

156 ft. 1⅜ in., throwing discus Olympic style,
veight 4 lbs. 6½ oz. (8 ft. 2½ in. circle), James
)uncan, May 27, 1912.

Throwing Same from 7-foot Circle.

145 ft. 9½ in., James Duncan, June 2, 1912.

Throwing Same from 8 ft. 2½ in. Circle, Right and Left Hand.

252 ft. 8⅞ in., James Duncan, May 27, 1912.

Throwing the Discus Greek Style.

116 ft. 7½ in., M. J. Sheridan, June 6, 1908.

WORLD'S RECORDS ATHLETICS—
WOMEN

30 yds. run., .03 3/5, Betty Brown, New Haven Nor. Sch. of Gym.

50 yds. run, .06, Eleanor Macbeth, New Haven Nor. Sch. of Gym.

75 yds. run, .08 3/5, L. Haydock, Bryn Mawr College.

100 yds. run, .11 3/5, Miss Lines, at Paris, France.

220 yds. run, .30 3/5, Francesca King, Wykeham Rise School.

60 yds. hurdle (4 hurdles, 2 ft. 6 in. high), .09 1/5, F. Crenshaw, E. Faries, Bryn Mawr College.

60 yds. hurdles (4 hurdles, 2 ft. high), .09 1/5, Gertrude Rath, Hollins College.

65 yds. hurdle (6 hurdles, 2 ft. 6 in. high), .11, Mary Worrall, Sargent Sch. for Phys. Ed.

100 yds. hurdles (8 hurdles, 2 ft. 6 in. high), .15 2/5, Mary C. Morgan, Bryn Mawr College.

100 yds. hurdles (8 hurdles, 2 ft. high), .15 1/5, Florieda Batson, Rosemary Hall.

Relay race, 220 yds. (4 runners), .30 3/5, Mildred Carl, Winifred Allen, Celestine Igoe, Ruth Griswold, New Haven Nor. Sch. of Gym.

Relay race, 440 yds. (4 runners), 1.1 1/5, Ball, Lefebvre, Hensen, Hadley, Long Beach (Cal.) High School.

Running high jump, 4 ft. 9 in., D. Horner, St. Mary's Hall.

Standing high jump, 3 ft. 8 in., Natalie Wilson, Sargent Sch. for Phys. Ed.

Running broad jump, 16 ft. 9½ in., Maude Devereux, Skidmore Sch. of Arts.

Standing broad jump, 8 ft. 10 in., Esther Rountree, Hollins College.

Running hop, step and jump, 33 ft. 6 in., Ellen V. Hayes, Sweet Briar College.

Pole vault, 7 ft. 2 in., Mildred Carl, New Haven Nor. Sch. of Gym.

Putting 6-lb. shot, 43 ft., Leslie Perkins, Sargent Sch. of Phys. Ed.

Putting 8-lb. shot, 34 ft. 1⅞ in., Frances Jackling, University of California.

Putting 12-lb. shot, 28 ft. 4 in., Margaret Mitchell, Wykeham Rise School.

Throwing the discus (free style), Nell Carroll, Florida State College for Women, 98 ft. 2 in.

Throwing the javelin, 98 ft. 2½ in., Rhea Reidel, Sargent Sch. for Phys. Ed.

Throwing baseball, 218 ft. 5 in., Mabel Hale, Dwight Indian Training School.

Throwing the basketball, 89 ft. 6 in., Maud Rosenbaum, Oakesmere School.

Throwing the hurl ball, 85 ft. 4½ in., M. Scattergood, Bryn Mawr College.

Throwing the small hurl ball, 112 ft. 7 in., Nell Carroll, Florida State College.

WORLD'S SWIMMING RECORDS— AMATEUR—BATH

50 yds., D. P. Kahanamoku, .23 2/5, Aug. 6, 1913.

100 yds., John Weissmuller, .53 1/5, Aug. 12, 1921.

100 metres, Norman Ross, 1.01.

120 yards, P. McGillivray, 1.08 2/5.

150 yards, T. Cann, 1.29 3/5.

200 yards, Norman Ross, 2.06 2/5.

200 metres, Norman Ross, 2.21 3/5.

220 yards, Norman Ross, 2.20 1/5.

300 yards, Norman Ross, 3.16 3/5.

400 metres, Norman Ross, 5.05 3/5.

440 yards, Norman Ross, 5.03 4/5.

500 metres, Ludy Langer, 6.48 2/5, Nov. 12, 1921.

500 yards, Norman Ross, 5.53 2/5.

880 yards, Norman Ross, 10.55 2/5.

1000 yards, Norman Ross, 12.38 2/5.

1320 yards, C. M. Daniels, 17.45 4/5.

One mile, Norman Ross, 22.38 1/5.

Two miles, Geo. Read, 54.54.

1000 metres, M. Annebourg (free style), 14.19, Christiania, Norway, Aug. 21, 1921.

WORLD'S SWIMMING RECORDS— AMATEUR—OPEN WATER

50 yards, D. P. Kahanamoku, .23.

100 yards, D. P. Kahanamoku, .53.

100 yards, Warren Kealoha, .53, 1921.

100 metres, D. P. Kahanamoku, 1.00 4/5.

120 yards, D. P. Kahanamoku, 1.07 2/5.

150 yards, D. P. Kahanamoku, 1.32.

200 metres, P. McGillivray, 2.24 1/5.

220 yards, P. McGillivray, 2.21 1/5.

300 yards, B. Kieran, 3.31 4/5.

400 metres, Ludy Langer, 5.17.

440 yards, Ludy Langer, 5.17.

500 metres, G. R. Hodgson, 7.06.

500 yards, Ludy Langer, 6.11 2/5.

880 yards, H. Taylor, 11.25 2/5.

1000 yards, Ludy Langer, 13.07 2/5.

1320 yards, W. Longworth, 17.42.

One mile, G. R. Hodgson, 23.34½.

Two miles, W. Longworth, 51.32.

1000 metres, G. R. Hodgson, 14.37.

1500 metres, G. R. Hodgson, 22.00.

WORLD'S RECORDS SWIMMING— BACKSTROKE—AMATEUR

100 yards, Warren Kealoha, 1.06, 1921.

150 yards, Warren Kealoha, 1.47 2/5, 1921.

WORLD'S SWIMMING RECORDS— PROFESSIONAL

100 yards, 1.01½, J. Nuttall, Sept. 26, 1893.

150 yards, 1.39, D. Billington, Aug. 24, 1907.

200 yards, 2.18½, D. Billington, Oct. 2, 1906.

220 yards, 2.37, J. Nuttall, Nov. 6, 1894; (recog-
ized in Australia) Oscar Dickman, March 11,
911, 2.32.

300 yards, 3.32 1/5, D. Billington, Sept. 20, 1905.

440 yards, 5.26, D. Billington, Oct. 27, 1906.

500 yards, 6.06, D. Billington, Sept. 18, 1905.

500 yards, 7.20 (open water), J. Nuttall, Sept. 2, 1893.

800 yards, 11.04½, J. Nuttall, England, Oct. 16, 1890.

880 yards, 11.37, D. Billington, Oct. 10, 1906; 11.18, Oscar Dickman, March 11, 1911.

1000 yards, 12.45, D. Billington, Sept. 19, 1905.

¾ mile, 17.36 2/5, David Billington, April 14, 1907.

1 mile, 26.08, J. Nuttall (open water), Aug. 19, 1893; (110 yard course), Dave Billington, Aug. 2, 1913, 24.11 1/5.

20⅜ miles, 5 hrs. 51 min., Fred Cavill, July 6, 1876.

34 miles, 9 hrs. 39 min., J. Wolfe, Aug. 7, 1905.

35 miles, 21 hrs. 45 min., Capt. Matthew Webb, Dover, England, to Calais, Aug. 24-25, 1875.

40 miles, 9 hrs. 57 min., Capt. Matthew Webb, with tide, River Thames, July 12, 1878.

74 miles, 84 hrs., Capt. Webb (restricted to 14 hrs. a day), Lambeth Baths, England, May 19, 1879. Drowned in Niagara Rapids, July 24, 1883.

T. W. Burgess swam English channel, Dover to Cape Grisnez, Sept. 6-7, 1911, 22 hrs. 35 min.

Capt. Alfred Brown, of Life Guards, swam from Battery, New York, to Sandy Hook, Aug. 28, 1913, 13 hrs. 38 min. He also swam through Panama Canal (48 miles) at opening in 1914.

WORLD'S SWIMMING RECORDS— AMATEUR—WOMEN—BATH

100 yards, 1.03 2/5, Ethelda Bleibtrey, 1921.

150 yards, 2.10 1/5, Ethelda Bleibtrey, March 17, 1920.

220 yards, 2.47 2/5, Charlotte Boyle, 1921.

300 yards, 4.17, Frances C. Cowells, Aug. 4, 1918.

440 yards, 6.30 1/5, Frances C. Cowells, Aug. 4, 1918.

500 yards, 7.19 3/5, Frances C. Cowells, June 28, 1919.

880 yards, 13.46 2/5, Frances C. Cowells, Aug. 26, 1918.

1000 yards, 16.50 2/5, Claire Galligan, Aug. 12, 1918.

One mile, 29.33 2/5, Claire Galligan, Aug. 12, 1918.

WORLD'S RECORD FOR PLUNGING
Man
82 ft. 9 in., Fred Schwedt (time limit 1 min.), March 1, 1920. *Woman*

66 ft., Charlotte Boyle, 1920.

WORLD'S RECORD SWIMMING— BACKSTROKE

100 yards, 1.16, Sybil Bauer, 1921.

150 yards, 2.06 4/5, Sybil Bauer, 1921.

WORLD'S RECORD HIGH DIVE

186 ft. 6 in., K. P. Speedy, at London, 1917-18, in tank 11½ ft. long, 8 ft. wide, 4½ ft. deep.

WORLD'S SWIMMING RECORDS—
AMATEUR—WOMEN—OPEN WATER

50 yards, .29 1/5, Frances C. Schroth, Nov. 3, 1919.

100 yards, 1.04 2/5, Ethelda Bleibtrey, April 17, 1920.

200 yards, 2.36 4/5, Ethelda Bleibtrey, Aug. 5, 1921.

220 yards, 2.55 2/5, Ethelda Bleibtrey, July 24, 1920.

440 yards, 6.21 3/5, Ethelda Bleibtrey, April 17, 1920.

500 yards, 7.32 3/5, Fanny Durack, Sydney, N. S. W.

880 yards, 12.52, Fanny Durack, Sydney, N. S. W.

1 mile, 26.08, Fanny Durack, Sydney, N. S. W.

WORLD'S RECORD RELAY RACE—
SWIMMING—WOMEN

400 yards, 4 min. 47 sec. (Misses Ethelda Bleibtrey, Charlotte Boyle; Aileen Riggin and Helen Wainwright), Aug. 12, 1921.

WORLD'S RECORDS IN BOXING

1719—Boxing was first inaugurated in England.

1719—James Figg, England, first champion. Held title eleven years.

1732—James Broughton, held title eighteen years.

1743—First set of gloves used in boxing exhibition.

1743—First set of boxing rules framed by James Broughton, Aug. 10.

1865—The present boxing rules were introduced by the Marquis of Queensbury (England).

1816—First prizefight in America (Jacob Hyer beat Tom Beasly).

1882—John L. Sullivan, first world's champion, Marquis of Queensbury rules, defeating Paddy Ryan, 9 rounds, Feb. 7.

Longest Fight

6 hrs. 15 min. (Prize Ring rules), Jim Kelly vs. Jonathan Smith, Melbourne, Australia, November, 1855.

Longest Fight in U. S.
(Bare Knuckles)

4 hrs. 20 min., A. J. Fitzpatrick vs. James O'Neill, Berwick, Maine, Dec. 4, 1860.

Longest Fight in Canada
(Bare Knuckles)

2 hrs. 58 min. (152 rounds), Dominick Bradley vs. S. S. Rankin, Port Abino, Can.

Longest Fight by Rounds

276, Patsey Tunney vs. Jack Jones, Cheshire, England, 1825.

Shortest Fights

2 seconds, Battling Nelson vs. Wm. Rossler, at Harvey, Ill., April 5, 1902.

18 seconds, Jack Dempsey vs. Fred Fulton, 1920.

21 seconds, Micky McCabe vs. Joe Steers, New York City, Dec. 9, 1921.

30 seconds, Head vs. Cannon, Carbondale, Pa., May 23, 1886 (bare knuckles).

Longest Glove Contest

(Queensbury Rules)

7 hrs. 19 min. (110 rounds), Andy Burke vs. Jack Burke, April 6, 1893.

WORLD'S UNDEFEATED BOXING CHAMPIONS

Jack McAuliffe, 1893-1899 (lightweight champion, retired).

John L. Sullivan, retired as champion bare knuckles, won from Jake Kilrain, in Richburg, Miss., 75 rounds, July 8, 1889.

Jas. J. Jeffries, 1899-1905 (retired heavyweight champion).

WORLD'S RECORD FOR CONSECUTIVE KNOCK-OUTS

21, Stanley Ketchel, from May, 1905, to May, 1907.

WORLD'S CHAMPIONS REGAINING LOST TITLES

Stanley Ketchel, from Billy Papke (middleweight).

Jack Britton, from Ted ("Kid") Lewis (welterweight).

Pete Herman, from Joe Lynch (bantamweight).

WORLD'S NOTED RING BATTLES
(25 rounds and over)

25 rounds, Jeffries defeated Sharkey, Nov. 3, 1899.

25 rounds, Ben Jordan defeated Geo. Dixon, July 1, 1898.

26 rounds, Jess Willard defeated Jack Johnson, April 5, 1915.

27 rounds, Jack Dempsey defeated Jack Fogerty, Feb. 3, 1886.

28 rounds, Jack McAuliffe defeated Harry Gilmore, Jan. 14, 1887.

35 rounds, Billy Edwards defeated Arthur Chambers, Sept. 4, 1872.

40 rounds, Ad. Wolgast defeated Bat Nelson, Feb. 22, 1910.

42 rounds, Joe Gans defeated Bat Nelson (foul), Sept. 3, 1906.

43 rounds, Jimmy Dunn defeated Bill Davis, May 16, 1865.

61 rounds, Jim Corbett vs. Peter Jackson (draw), May 21, 1891.

74 rounds, Jack McAuliffe vs. Jean Carney (draw), Nov. 16, 1887.

75 rounds, John L. Sullivan vs. Jake Kilrain, July 8, 1889.

87 rounds, Paddy Ryan vs. Joe Goss, May 30, 1880.

136 rounds, Arthur Chambers vs. John Clarke, March 27, 1879.

WORLD'S RECORDS IN BILLIARDS
Straight Rail (5x10 table)
2634 points, Catton, Chicago, Feb. 25, 1916.

Straight Rail (4½x9 table)

3001 points, Wallace Phares, Clinton, Iowa (amateur), 1915.

3000 points, Jake Schaefer, San Francisco, Cal.

Best Average (5x10 table)

333½ points, Jake Schaefer, Chicago, Ill.

Fourteen-inch Balk Line—Anchor In

566—Jake Schaefer, New York.

Best Average

100—Jake Schaefer, New York.
100—Frank Ives, Chicago.

Fourteen-inch Balk Line—Anchor Barred

359—Frank Ives, Chicago.

Best Average

63 1/3—Frank Ives, New York.

14-inch Balk Line—One Shot In

303—Willie Hoppe, New York, April 23, 1914.

Best Average

40—Willie Hoppe, New York, April 23, 1914.

14-inch Balk Line—One Shot In—Amateur

170—Calvin Demarest, Chicago, March 17, 1908.

Best Average

57 1/7—Calvin Demarest, Chicago, March 17, 1908.

18-inch Balk Line

200—Frank Ives, New York.

Best Average
50—Frank Ives, New York.

18-inch Balk Line—No Shot In
111—Jake Schaefer, Chicago.
Best Average
19 3/13—Frank Ives, Chicago.

18-inch Balk Line—2 Shots In (500 Points)
Best Average
135¼—Willie Hoppe, Chicago, 1914.

1500 Points—Three Nights
Best Average
55 15/27—Willie Hoppe, Chicago, 1914.

High Runs
480—Jake Schaefer, Chicago, Oct. 21, 1921.
436—Jake Schaefer, New York City, March 5, 1921.
Best Average (400 points)
126 4/5—Jake Schaefer, New York, March 5, 1921 (Day's play 800 points).
129¼—Jake Schaefer, New York, March 5, 1921.

Best Average for Match (4800 points)
50-50-95—Edouard Horemans, New York, March 27, 1921.

18-inch Balk Line—1 Shot In
157—Willie Hoppe, Chicago, March 5, 1908.
Best Average
33 1/3—Willie Hoppe, New York City, Dec. 7, 1910.

3 Cushion Caroms

50 points (31 innings)—Joe Carney, Denver, Col., Jan. 5, 1912.

High Run

18—Pierre Maupome, St. Louis, Mo., Sept. 18, 1914.

18—Charles Morin, St. Louis, Mo., May 20, 1915.

25—Willie Hoppe (exhibition), San Francisco, Jan. 8, 1918.

WORLD'S RECORD POCKET BILLIARDS

137—Ralph Greenleaf, unfinished run (under new rules), Camden, N. J., March 15, 1918.

WORLD'S RECORD EXHIBITION GAMES

Billiards 18-2

1009—W. W. Spink, Los Angeles, Cal., Oct. 12, 1912.

702—Ed. Horemans vs. Ed. Knowles, New York.

308—W. Hoppe, New York City.

WORLD'S BOWLING RECORDS

Individual—Open

Three Games

Roy Flagg, Aberdeen, So. Dak., 270-300-300. Total 870. Average 290.

Wm. E. Roach, Wilmington, Del., 300, 300, 269. Total 869.   Average 289 2/3 (1906).

Six Games
Lee R. Johns, Newark, N. J. (1909), 279, 268, 248, 277, 277, 279.   Total 1628.   Average 271 1/3.

All Events
James Smith, Buffalo, N. Y. (9 games), averaged 228 8/9 at Toronto, Can., 1912.   Total 2060.

Mortimer Lindsey, New Haven, Ct., 9 games, averaged 225 6/9 at Paterson, N. J., 1912. Total 2031.

Head Pin
118 pins.   Oscar Steinquest at New York, 1909.

Tournament
Three Games
Chas. Schaeder, Brooklyn, N. Y., 267, 279, 278. Total 824.   Average 271 1/3 (1907).

Six Games
Chas. Schaeder, Brooklyn, N. Y., 236, 255, 267, 279, 263, 232.   Total 1537.   Average 256 1/6. (1907)

Seventy-five Games
Fred B. Egelhoff, Brooklyn, N. Y.   Average 230.29 (1906).

Greatest Number of 300 Scores
12—John Koster, New York.

Highest Woman Score
277—Mrs. Nellie Lester, New York, 1909.

Two Men—Open
537—Knox-Satterthwaite, Philadelphia, Pa., Feb. 18, 1912.

Three Games

1445—Knox-Satterthwaite, Philadelphia, Pa. Feb. 18, 1912. .

Tournament

523—McGuirk-Grady, Rochester, N. Y., 1908.

Three Games

1318—McGuirk-Grady, Rochester, N. Y., 1908.

Three Men—Open

757—Lindsey-Riddell-Dunbar, at New York, 1908.

Tournament

748—Imperial Team (Brooklyn Palace Tournament), 1910.

Five Men (Open)—All Wooden Balls

1175—Algonquins, New York (Columbia Alley), 1906.

1290—Vermonts, Chicago, 1917.

Three Games

1126—Brooklyn Interstate Team, Brooklyn, 1905.
3497—Rochester State League Team (Rochester), Jan. 21, 1913. Average 1,165.2.

Four Games

4496—Rochester State League Team (Rochester), Jan. 21, 1913. Average 1124.

Tournament

1207—Howard Majors team, Chicago, Ill., 1907.
1207—Koenig & Kaiser team, St. Louis, Mo., 1908.
1207—Burkes team, St. Louis, Mo., 1909.

Three Games
1124—Howard Majors team, Chicago, Ill., 1906.

Head Pin
545 pins—Roseville A. A., Newark, N. J., 1909.

Six Consecutive Games
51 strikes, 9 spares, no splits or errors, Lee Johns, Newark, N. J., Dec. 10, 1909.

LONGEST PERIOD CHESS CHAMPION
28 years, William Steinitz, 1866-1894.

27 years, Dr. Emanuel Lasker, 1894-1921.

WORLD'S FOOTBALL RECORDS
Ivan Grone (Kendall College), kicked 61 goals, ollowing touchdowns, 1916.

Long Distance Kick from Placement
65 yards (field goal), J. T. Haxall, 1882.

62 yards (field goal), Pat O'Dea, Wisconsin vs. J. W. U., 1898.

Players Who Kicked 50 Yards and Over
65 yards, J. T. Haxall (Princeton) vs. Yale, Jov. 30, 1882.

63 yards, M. Payne (Dakota Wes.) vs. N. W. Jor., Oct. 16, 1915.

62 yards, P. J. O'Dea (Wisconsin) vs. Northwestern, Nov. 25, 1898.

62 yards, Geo. Gipp (Notre Dame) vs. Western les., Oct. 7, 1916.

58 yards, J. P. Davis (Dickinson) vs. Pittsburgh, Nov. 25, 1905.

55 yards, J. V. Cowling (Harvard) vs. Princeton, Nov. 17, 1883.

55 yards, J. E. Duffy (Michigan) vs. Cornell, Nov. 21, 1891.

55 yards, W. G. Crowell (Swarthmore) vs. F. and M., Nov. 5, 1904.

55 yards, Fred Bennion (Utah) vs. Utah Agri. Coll., Nov. 27, 1904.

55 yards, O. W. Wilcox (Mansfield Normal) vs. Wyoming, Oct. 24, 1906.

53 yards, G. S. McCaa (Lafayette) vs. Brown, Oct. 24, 1908.

53 yards, G. J. O'Brien, Mt. Union vs. Allegheny, Oct. 31, 1908.

53 yards, O. L. Guernsey, Yale vs. Princeton, Nov. 13, 1915.

52 yards, D. B. Pratt, Alabama vs. Clemson, Oct. 23, 1909.

52 yards, W. J. O'Brien, Iowa vs. Minnesota, Oct. 28, 1911.

52 yards, Carl Woodward, Tulane vs. St. Louis, Nov. 1, 1913.

50 yards, Alex Moffatt, Princeton vs. Harvard, Nov. 17, 1883.

50 yards, John Baird, Princeton vs. Navy, Oct. 9, 1897.

50 yards, P. J. O'Dea, Wisconsin vs. Chicago, Nov. 13, 1897.

50 yards, C. D. Daly, Army vs. Yale, Nov. 2, 1901.

50 yards, J. R. DeWitt, Princeton vs. Cornell, Nov. 1, 1902.

50 yards, J. R. DeWitt, Princeton vs. Yale, Nov. ·15, 1902.

50 yards, T. S. Cusack, N. Y. Univ. vs. Rens-elaer, Oct. 24, 1914.

50 yards, S. L. Cofall, Notre Dame vs. Car-isle, Oct. 24, 1914.

50 yards, J. L. Cody, Vanderbilt vs. Virginia, Oct. 28, 1916.

Players Making Runs of 100 Yards or More

110 yards, G. S. McCaa, Lafayette vs. Swart., Oct. 15, 1909.

109 yards, G. C. Gray, Oberlin vs. Cornell, Oct. 10, 1908.

108 yards, Erehart, Indiana vs. Iowa, Oct. 27, 1912.

106 yards, W. H. Eckersall, Chicago vs. Wis., Nov. 26, 1904.

105 yards, H. M. Coleman, Wis. vs. Minn., Oct. 24, 1891.

105 yards, Sherman, California vs. Stanford, Nov. 8, 1902.

105 yards, Chas. Dillon, Carlisle vs. Harvard, Oct. 31, 1903.

105 yards, W. E. Sprackling, Brown vs. Car-lisle, Nov. 20, 1909.

105 yards, R. O. Ainslee, Williams vs. Cornell, Nov. 4, 1911.

103 yards, W. B. Richardson, Brown vs. Prince-ton, Nov. 4, 1899.

101 yards, R. W. Richardson, Pitts. vs. Buck., Oct. 26, 1908.

101 yards, C. Medsker, Case vs. Mt. Union, Nov. 6, 1919.

100 yards, R. W. Watson, Yale vs. Harvard, Nov. 12, 1881.

100 yards, H. R. Flanders, Yale vs. Harvard, Nov. 22, 1884.

100 yards, E. G. Bray, Lafayette vs. U. of Pa., Oct. 21, 1899.

100 yards, Arthur Poe, Princeton vs. Yale, Nov. 12, 1898.

100 yards, E. B. Cochems, Wis. vs. Chicago, Nov. 28, 1901.

100 yards, G. Bailey, Maine vs. Bowdoin, Oct. 31, 1903.

100 yards, W. P. Steffen, Chicago vs. Wis., Nov. 21, 1908.

100 yards, Gustave Welch, Carl. vs. U. of Pa., Nov. 11, 1911.

WORLD'S RECORD MOTOR PACED BICYCLES—COMPETITION

1 mile, 1.09 1/5, Hugh McLean, Aug. 27, 1903.

2 miles, 2.19, Hugh McLean, Aug. 27, 1903.

3 miles, 3.31 3/5, James Moran, June 28, 1904.

4 miles, 4.43, H. Caldwell, Sept. 1, 1903.

4 miles, 4.43, R. A. Walthour, May 31, 1904.

5 miles, 5.51, R. A. Walthour, May 31, 1904.

6 miles, 7.00 1/5, R. A. Walthour, May 31, 1904.

7 miles, 8.07 3/5, R. A. Walthour, May 31, 1904.

8 miles, 9.14 1/5, R. A. Walthour, May 31, 1904.

9 miles, 10.22, R. A. Walthour, May 31, 1904.

10 miles, 11.29 1/5, R. A. Walthour, May 31, 1904.

11 miles, 12.36 1/5, R. A. Walthour, May 31, 1904.

12 miles, 13.43, R. A. Walthour, May 31, 1904.

13 miles, 14.50 2/5, R. A. Walthour, May 31, 1904.

14 miles, 15.57 1/5, R. A. Walthour, May 31, 1904.

15 miles, 17.03 2/5, R. A. Walthour, May 31, 1904.

16 miles, 18.10 3/5, R. A. Walthour, May 31, 1904.

17 miles, 19.17 2/5, R. A. Walthour, May 31, 1904.

18 miles, 20.24 1/5, R. A. Walthour, May 31, 1904.

19 miles, 21.30 4/5, R. A. Walthour, May 31, 1904.

20 miles, 22.37 3/5, R. A. Walthour, May 31, 1904.

21 miles, 23.44 3/5, R. A. Walthour, May 31, 1904.

22 miles, 24.51 4/5, R. A. Walthour, May 31, 1904.

23 miles, 25.59, R. A. Walthour, May 31, 1904.

24 miles, 27.07 3/5, R. A. Walthour, May 31, 1904.

25 miles, 28.15 1/5, R. A. Walthour, May 31, 1904.

26 miles, 29.22 3/5, R. A. Walthour, May 31, 1904.

27 miles, 30.30 1/5, R. A. Walthour, May 31, 1904.

28 miles, 31.37 2/5, R. A. Walthour, May 31, 1904.

29 miles, 32.48, R. A. Walthour, May 31, 1904.

30 miles, 33.52 3/5, R. A. Walthour, May 31, 1904.

31 miles, 36.26, H. Caldwell, Sept. 1, 1903.

32 miles, 37.37 1/5, H. Caldwell, Sept. 1, 1903.

33 miles, 38.48 4/5, H. Caldwell, Sept. 1, 1903.

34 miles, 39.57 3/5, H. Caldwell, Sept. 1, 1903.

35 miles, 41.07 3/5, H. Caldwell, Sept. 1, 1903.

36 miles, 42.18 1/5, H. Caldwell, Sept. 1, 1903.

37 miles, 43.28 1/5, H. Caldwell, Sept. 1, 1903.

38 miles, 44.39 1/5, H. Caldwell, Sept. 1, 1903.

39 miles, 45.49 2/5, H. Caldwell, Sept. 1, 1903.

40 miles, 47.00, H. Caldwell, Sept. 1, 1903.

41 miles, 48.10 4/5, H. Caldwell, Sept. 1, 1903.

42 miles, 49.21 1/5, H. Caldwell, Sept. 1, 1903.

43 miles, 50.31 1/5, H. Caldwell, Sept .1, 1903.

44 miles, 51.41 1/5, H. Caldwell, Sept. 1, 1903.

45 miles, 52.50 4/5, H. Caldwell, Sept. 1, 1903.

46 miles, 54.23 4/5, H. Caldwell, Sept. 1, 1903.

47 miles, 55.49 3/5, H. Caldwell, Sept. 1, 1903.

48 miles, 57.21 1/5, H. Caldwell, Sept. 1, 1903.

49 miles, 58.43 1/5, H. Caldwell, Sept. 1, 1903.

50 miles, 59.59, H. Caldwell, Sept. 1, 1903.

100 miles, 2.48.11 4/5, H. Caldwell, Sept. 8, 1904.

World's Record Fastest Mile (Paced)

1.06 1/5—R. A. Walthour, May 31, 1904.

Against Time (Paced)

1/4 mile, 0.18 4/5, S. H. Wilcox, June 18, 1913.

1/3 mile, 0.27 4/5, J. S. Johnson, Oct. 29, 1896.

1/2 mile, 0.37 3/5, S. H. Wilcox, June 8, 1913.

2/3 mile, 0.55, Ray Duer, Aug. 28, 1910.

1 mile, 1.04 1/5, Menus Bedell, June 30, 1917.

2 miles, 2.09 4/5, Ray Duer, June 27, 1909.

3 miles, 3.13 2/5, Menus Bedell, June 30. 1917.

4 miles, 4.16 4/5, Menus Bedell, June 30, 1917.

5 miles, 5.18 2/5, Menus Bedell, June 30, 1917.

6 miles, 6.28 1/5, Ray Duer, June 27, 1909.

7 miles, 7.33 3/5, Ray Duer, June 27, 1909.

8 miles, 8.38 1/5, Ray Duer, June 27, 1909.

9 miles, 9.45 4/5, Ray Duer, June 27, 1909.

10 miles, 10.59 3/5, Menus Bedell, July 7, 1917.

On June 3, 1910, Geo. Kramer, paced by auto, made one mile in 58 seconds on one mile circular board track.

WORLD'S BICYCLE RECORDS—UN-PACED—IN COMPETITION

1/4 mile, 0.27 2/5, F. L. Kramer, July 4, 1915.

1/2 mile, 0.36 3/5, F. L. Kramer, May 23, 1915.

1/2 mile, 0.53, F. L. Kramer, July 4, 1917.

2/3 mile, 1.10 4/5, Alfred Grenda, Aug. 11, 1915.

3/4 mile, 1.21, F. L. Kramer, July 5, 1907.

1 mile, 1.45, R. McNamara, Sept. 17, 1916.

2 miles, 3.38 1/5, A. J. Clarke, Aug. 2, 1910.

3 miles, 5.35 3/5, Ivor Lawson, July 25, 1906.

4 miles, 7.42 2/5, Wm. Hanley, July 7, 1915.

5 miles, 9.30, R. McNamara, July 23, 1919.

10 miles, 20.07 1/5, R. McNamara, Aug. 16, 1916.

15 miles, 31.28 2/5, R. McNamara, Aug. 20, 1916.

20 miles, 42.23 2/5, P. Drobach, Aug. 8, 1917.

25 miles, 53.38 2/5, R. McNamara, Sept. 22, 1915.

50 miles, 1.49 4/5, Alfred Goullet, Aug. 19, 1920.

Against Time—Unpaced

1/6 mile, 0.15 2/5, Al. Krebs, July 4, 1911.

1/4 mile, 0.23 4/5, Ivor Lawson, July 4, 1906.

1/3 mile, 0.33, A. J. Clarke, July 24, 1912.

1/2 mile, 0.50 2/5, A. J. Clarke, Aug. 24, 1908.

2/3 mile, 1.11 1/5, Alfred Goullet, June 17, 1912.

3/4 mile, 1.24 3/5, Alfred Goullet, July 1, 1912.

1 mile, 1.51, Alfred Goullet, July 1, 1912.

2 miles, 4.01 3/5, E. A. Pye, Aug. 28, 1910.

3 miles, 6.09 1/5, E. A. Pye, Aug. 28, 1910.

4 miles, 8.34 3/5, S. Williams, July 30, 1909.

5 miles, 10.38, S. Williams, July 30, 1909.

10 miles, 23.09 2/5, W. Hamilton, July 9, 1898.

15 miles, 35.03, W. Hamilton, July 9, 1898.

20 miles, 47.08 2/5, W. Hamilton, July 9, 1898.

25 miles, 59.13 2/5, W. Hamilton, July 9, 1898.

WORLD'S RECORDS—MOTORCYCLES —TRACK

1 mile, .33 2/5, Walker, Feb. 22, 1921.

2 miles, 1.12 4/5, Humiston, Dec. 30, 1912.

5 miles, 3.06 4/5, Humiston, Dec. 30, 1912.

10 miles, 6.18, Humiston, Dec. 30, 1912.

25 miles, 16.27, Seymour, May 17, 1912.

50 miles, 29.34, Walker, Feb. 22, 1921.

100 miles, 1.07.43, Walker, Sept. 12, 1915.

200 miles, 2.26.48, Jones, July 5, 1920.

300 miles, 3.30.20, Goudy, Sept. 12, 1915.

500 miles, 6.59.15, Baker, Aug. 14, 1917.

1000 miles, 16.14.15, Baker, Aug. 15, 1917.

WORLD'S RECORDS—MOTORCYCLES —ROAD

1 mile, .35, Jack Booth, Oct. 7, 1916.

5 miles, 3.15 2/5, Ray Creviston, Mar. 23, 1919.

25 miles, 21.56, L. G. Buckner, April 26, 1920.

50 miles, 40.01, Gene Walker, April 26, 1920.

100 miles, 1.22.11.98, Albert Burns, Sept. 6, 1920.

200 miles, 2.48.37.12, Ray Weishear, Sept. 6, 1920.

300 miles, 5.02.32.00, Lee Taylor, Nov. 26, 1914.

500 miles, 9.58.00.00, E. G. Baker, Feb., 1916.

1000 miles, 21.03.00.00, E. G. Baker, Feb., 1916.

WORLD'S RECORDS—MOTORCYCLES —DIRT TRACK

1 mile, .44 5/10, Fred Ludlow, Oct. 15, 1921.

2 miles, 1.38 4/5, Albert Burns, Sept. 7, 1919.

5 miles, 3.45.74, Fred Ludlow, Oct. 15, 1921.

10 miles, 7.38.80, Fred Ludlow, Oct. 15, 1921.

25 miles, 19.24 2/5, Fred Ludlow, Sept. 19, 1920.

50 miles, 40.11 3/5, De Simone, July 4, 1919.

100 miles, 1.28.06 2/5, Jim Davis, June 13, 1915.

WORLD'S RECORDS—MOTORCYCLES —BY HOURS

1 hour, 88 mi. 350 yds., Lee Humiston, Jan. 7, 1913.

2 hours, 134 mi. 880 yds., Morty Graves, July 18, 1909.

3 hours, 197 mi. 1271 yds., A. J. Moorhouse, April 18, 1912.

4 hours, 254 mi. 1638 yds., C. B. Franklin, June 20, 1912.

5 hours, 310 mi., C. B. Franklin, June 20, 1912.

14 hours, 641 mi., 587 yds., Chas. Spencer, Oct. 2, 1909.

15 hours, 677 mi. 587 yds., Chas. Spencer, Oct. 2, 1909.

16 hours, 730 mi., Chas. Spencer, Oct. 2, 1909.

17 hours, 767 mi. 587 yds., Chas. Spencer, Oct. 2, 1909.

18 hours, 812 mi. 587 yds., Chas. Spencer, Oct. 2, 1909.

19 hours, 862 mi. 587 yds., Chas. Spencer, Oct. 2, 1909.

20 hours, 911 mi., Chas. Spencer, Oct. 2, 1909.

21 hours, 945 mi. 587 yds., Chas. Spencer, Oct. 2, 1909.

22 hours, 986 mi. 1174 yds., Chas Spencer, Oct. 2, 1909.

23 hours, 1035 mi. 1174 yds., Chas. Spencer, Oct. 2, 1909.

24 hours, 1534¾ mi., E. G. Baker, Aug. 15, 1917.

WORLD'S RECORDS—AUTOMOBILES

Speedway—Non-stock

1¼ miles, .39 4/5, Jimmy Murphy, Dec. 11, 1921.

2 miles, 1.09.57, Louis Chevrolet, Frontenac, Sept. 3, 1917.

3 miles, 1.54.81, Resta, Peugeot, June 24, 1916.

4 miles, 2.14.22, Louis Chevrolet, Frontenac, Sept. 3, 1917.

5 miles, 2.56.35, Resta, Peugeot, July 15, 1916.

10 miles, 5.20.20, Milton, Duesenberg, June 14, 1919.

15 miles, 8.18.90, De Palma, Packard Special, Sept. 3, 1917.

20 miles, 10.50.20, De Palma, Packard Special, July 28, 1918.

25 miles, 14.12.72, De Palma, Packard Special, Sept. 3, 1917.

50 miles, 26.23.40, De Palma, Packard, June 14, 1919.

75 miles, 42.40.28, Louis Chevrolet, Frontenac, Sept. 3, 1917.

100 miles, 54.17.80, G. Chevrolet, Frontenac, July 4, 1919.

150 miles, 1.26.14.90, Mulford, Hudson, June 16, 1917.

200 miles, 1.55.11.05 Mulford, Hudson, June 16, 1917.

250 miles, 2.15.11½, Tommy Milton, Dec. 11, 1921.

300 miles, 2.55.32.23, Anderson, Stutz, Oct. 9, 1915.

350 miles, 3.24.42.99, Anderson, Stutz, Oct. 9, 1915.

400 miles, 4.04.48.98, Resta, Peugeot, June 26, 1915.

450 miles, 4.35.05.78, Resta, Peugeot, June 26, 1915.

500 miles, 5.07.26.00, Resta, Peugeot, June 26, 1915.

Non-stock—1 Mile Circular Track

10 miles, 8.16.40, Burman, Peugeot, Jan. 3, 1915.

15 miles, 12.23.20, Burman, Peugeot, Jan. 3, 1915.

20 miles, 16.25.60, Burman, Peugeot, Jan 3, 1915.

25 miles, 20.28.80, Burman, Peugeot, Jan. 3, 1915.

50 miles, 40.57.80, Burman, Peugeot, Jan. 3, 1915.

75 miles, 1.08.56.00, Burman, Peugeot, Oct. 22, 1914.

100 miles, 1.29.00.00, Hearne, Chevrolet Special, Nov. 8, 1909.

150 miles, 2.30.51.00, Wishart, Mercer, Aug. 25, 1912.

200 miles, 3.21.48.00, Mulford, Mason Special, July 4, 1913.

Non-stock—Straightaway

10 miles, 5.14.40, Brown, Benz, March 24, 1909.

20 miles, 13.11.92, Burman, Buick Bug, March 30, 1911.

50 miles, 35.52.31, Burman, Buick Bug, March 28, 1911.

100 miles, 1.12.45.20, Berbin, Renault, March 6, 1908.

150 miles, 1.55.18.00, Disbrow, Special, March 31, 1911.

200 miles, 2.34.12.00, Disbrow, Special, March 31, 1911.

250 miles, 3.14.55.00, Disbrow, Special, March 31, 1911.

300 miles, 3.53.33.50, Disbrow, Special, March 31, 1911.

Non-stock—Speedway—Hours

1 hour, 74 miles, Harroun, Marmon, April 16, 1910.

2 hours, 148 miles, Harroun, Marmon, April 16, 1910.

24 hours, 1491 miles, Verbeck and Hirch, Fiat, April 8, 1910.

Circular Dirt Track

24 hours, 1196 miles, Patschke and Mulford, Lozier, Oct. 15, 1909.

Straightaway

1 hour, 81.65 miles, Disbrow, Special, Mar. 28, 1911.

WORLD'S RECORDS SIX-DAY BICYCLE RACE

1 hour, 26 miles, 6 laps, Cameron & Kaiser, 1914.

2 hours, 50 miles, 9 laps, Cameron & Kaiser, 1914.

9 hours, 211 miles, 8 laps, Cameron & Kaiser, 1914.

14 hours, 321 miles, 7 laps, Moran & McNamara, 1914.

15 hours, 342 miles, 9 laps, Moran & McNamara, 1914.

16 hours, 365 miles, 1 lap, Goullet & Grenda, 1914.

23 hours, 516 miles, 8 laps, Fogler & Hill, 1914.

24 hours, 537 miles, 9 laps, Fogler & Hill, 1914.

25 hours, 558 miles, 3 laps, Lawrence & Magin, 1914.

26 hours, 577 miles, 3 laps, Clarke & Root, 1914.

30 hours, 663 miles, Piercy & M. Bedell, 1915.

32 hours, 706 miles, 1 lap, Lawson & Root, 1915.

39 hours, 801 miles, 5 laps, Lawrence & Magin, 1914.

48 hours, 1011 miles, 1 lap, Goullet & Grenda, 1914.

56 hours, 1159 miles, 5 laps, Anderson & Dupuy, 1916.

57 hours, 1173 miles, 9 laps, Eaton & Madden, 1915.

58 hours, 1191 miles, 7 laps, Walthour & Halstead, 1914.

59 hours, 1209 miles, 9 laps, Goullet & Grenda, 1914.

66 hours, 1346 miles, Fogler & Hill, 1914.

72 hours, 1468 miles, 5 laps, Goullet & Grenda, 1914.

75 hours, 1505 miles, 1 lap, Goullet & Grenda, 1914.

82 hours, 1637 miles, 9 laps, Goullet & Grenda, 1914.

83 hours, 1653 miles, 4 laps, Clarke & Root, 1914.

85 hours, 1687 miles, 8 laps, Moran & McNamara, 1914.

86 hours, 1705 miles, 9 laps, Lawson & Drobach, 1914.

96 hours, 1904 miles, 1 lap, Cameron & Kaiser, 1914.

98 hours, 1945 miles, 2 laps, Goullet & Grenda, 1914.

102 hours, 2019 miles, 9 laps, Goullet & Grenda, 1914.

104 hours, 2051 miles, 5 laps, Fogler & Hill, 1914.

107 hours, 2100 miles, 7 laps, Fogler & Hill, 1914.

110 hours, 2149 miles, 8 laps, Goullet & Grenda, 1914.

113 hours, 2206 miles, 3 laps, Lawson & Drobach, 1914.

118 hours, 2304 miles, 9 laps, Verri & Egg, 1914.

120 hours, 2349 miles, 2 laps, Moran & McNamara, 1914.

123 hours, 2412 miles, 1 lap, Lawson & Drobach, 1914.

126 hours, 2472 miles, Goullet & Grenda, 1914.

128 hours, 2506 miles, 4 laps, Cameron & Kaiser, 1914.

129 hours, 2523 miles, 7 laps, Fogler & Hill, 1914.

130 hours, 2541 miles, 2 laps, Goullet & Grenda, 1914.

131 hours, 2558 miles, Cameron & Kaiser, 1914.

133 hours, 2591 miles, 4 laps, Lawson & Drobach, 1914.

135 hours, 2629 miles, 2 laps, Moran & McNamara, 1914.

World's Record

2759 miles, 2 laps, Goullet & Grenda, 1914.

(A greater mileage—2770 miles, 8 laps, was made in 1915, by Walthour & Moran, but track when re-measured proved short.)

World's Best 6 Day Cyclist

Alfred Goullet, won 14 out of 19 six day races.

WORLD'S RECORD ICE SKATING— AMATEUR

50 yards, .04 4/5, Fred J. Robson, Feb. 28, 1916.

60 yards, .06, Fred J. Robson, Feb. 28, 1916.

75 yards, .07 4/5 (indoor), Fred J. Robson, Feb. 28, 1916.

75 yards, .08 1/5 (outdoor), Morris Wood, Jan. 10, 1905.

100 yards, .09 3/5 (outdoor), Morris Wood, Jan. 24, 1903.

150 yards, .15 7/8 (outdoor), Geo. D. Phillips, Jan. 27, 1883.

200 yards, .16 2/5, J. C. Hemment, Jan. 24, 1895.

220 yards, .18, Fred J. Robson, Jan. 31, 1911.

220 yards, .19 (outdoor), Morris Wood, Jan. 24, 1903.

300 yards, .25 2/5, Roy McWhirter, March 5, 1916.

440 yards, .35 1/5, H. P. Mosher, Jan. 1, 1896.

440 yards, .36 4/5 (indoor), Morris Wood, Feb. 23, 1907.

660 yards, .59 3/5, Morris Wood, Feb. 2, 1904.

880 yards, 1.15 3/5, Ben O'Sicky, March 1, 1916.

1320 yards, 2.04 1/5, Edmund Lamy (indoor), Jan. 10, 1910.

1 mile, 2.39 4/5, Rob. C. McLean, (Han'p), Jan. 25, 1913.

1 mile, 2.41 1/5, Morris Wood (open), Feb. 13, 1904.

1½ miles, 4.10, Lot Roe (indoor), Jan. 29, 1910.

3 miles, 8.45, Roy McWhirter, Feb. 12, 1921.

4 miles, 12.00½, A. Schiebe & J. Millson, Feb. 13, 1894.

5 miles, 14.55, Edmund Lamy (indoor), Feb., 1910.

10 miles, 32.51, Arthur J. Hess (indoor), Feb., 1911.

15 miles, 49.34 1/5, Arthur J. Hess (indoor), Feb., 1911.

25 miles, 1.30.15, John Karlson (aged 41), Feb. 6, 1916.

26 miles, 1.25.22, Archie Rogers, Feb., 1917.

Backward Skating

440 yds. (indoor), 46 sec., John Hoernig, Boston, Feb. 16, 1912.

WORLD'S RECORD ICE SKATING —AMATEUR (METERS)

200 meters (219 yds.), 19 2/5 sec., Oakley Bush, Davos, Switzerland, 1910.

500 meters (547 yds.), 43 2/5 sec., Oskar Mathiesen, Davos, Switzerland, Jan. 17, 1914.

600 meters (656 yds.), 59 3/5 sec., Morris Wood, Feb. 13, 1904.

1000 meters (1,093 yds.), 1 min., 31 4/5 sec., P. Oestlund, Davos, Switzerland, 1910.

1,500 meters (1,640 yds.), 2 min., 17 2/5 sec., Oskar Mathiesen, Davos, Switzerland, Jan. 8, 1914.

5,000 meters (3 miles, 188 yds.), 8 min., 36 2/5 sec., Oskar Mathiesen, Davos, Switzerland, Jan. 17, 1914.

10,000 meters (6 miles, 374 yds.), 17 min., 22 3/5 sec., Oskar Mathiesen, Stockholm, Sweden, Feb. 1, 1913.

Hurdle Jumping

220 yds., 6 hurdles, 27 in. high, 23 4/5 sec., Edmund Horton, Saranac Lake, N. Y., Jan. 30, 1913.

220 yds., 6 hurdles, 28 in. high, 25 sec., Fred J. Robson, Montreal, Canada, 1911.

Barrel Jumping

Morris Woods (amateur) jumped over 12 barrels in a row, 1912; Edmund Lamy (professional) jumped over 12 barrels in a row, Saranac Lake, N. Y., Jan. 30, 1913.

Jumping Records on Ice

Running high jump backward, 3 ft. 5½ in., S. H. Leweck, Chicago, Feb. 7, 1911.

Running high jump forward, 4 ft. 3 in., William H. Quinn, Boston, Jan. 31, 1911.

Running broad jump forward—25 ft. 7 in., Edmund Lamy, Saranac Lake, N. Y., Jan. 30, 1913.

WORLD'S RECORDS ICE SKATING— PROFESSIONAL

50 yards, .06, S. D. See and C. B. Davidson, Dec. 28, 1885.

75 yards, .08 3/5, S. D. See, Dec. 28, 1885.

100 yards, .09 4/5, John S. Johnson, 1893.

120 yards, .11 3/5, John S. Johnson, 1893.

200 yards, .17 2/5, John S. Johnson, Feb. 26, 1893.

440 yards, .31¼, John S. Johnson (straight-away), Jan. 23, 1894.

600 yards, .55 3/5, O. Rudd, May 5, 1893.

½ mile, 1.00 2/5, John S. Johnson, Dec. 28, 1897.

½ mile, 1.00 2/5, John Nilsson (outdoor track), Jan. 4, 1897.

½ mile, 1.16 1/5, Narval Baptie (indoor track), Jan. 10, 1908.

880 yards, 1.15, Bobby McLean, Feb. 16, 1918.·

2/3 mile, 1.54 4/5, O. Rudd, Jan. 25, 1895.

¾ mile, 1.55, J. S. Johnson (flying start—straight), February, 1898.

¾ mile, 2.13, J. S. Johnson (on track), Feb. 26, 1894.

1 mile, 2.35, Arthur Staff, Feb. 19, 1916.

1¼ miles, 3.43, John S. Johnson, Feb. 26, 1894.

1 1/3 miles, 3.48 1/5, O. Rudd, Jan. 25, 1895.

1½ miles, 4.28, John S. Johnson, Feb. 26, 1894.

1 2/3 miles, 4.45 4/5, O. Rudd, Jan. 24, 1895.

1¾ miles, 5.14, John S. Johnson, Feb. 26, 1894.

2 miles, 5.33 4/5, John Nilsson, Feb. 4, 1900.

2½ miles, 7.32, John S. Johnson, Feb. 26, 1894.

3 miles, 8.41 1/5, John Nilsson, Feb. 4, 1900.

3½ miles, 10.39, John S. Johnson, Feb. 26, 1894.

4 miles, 12.00 1/5, John Nilsson, Feb. 5, 1897.

4½ miles, 13.51, John S. Johnson, Feb. 26, 1894.

5 miles, 14.24, O. Rudd, Feb. 20, 1896.

6 miles, 18.38, John S. Johnson, Feb. 26, 1894.

7 miles, 21.43, John S. Johnson, Feb. 26, 1894.

8 miles, 24.55, John S. Johnson, Feb. 26, 1894.

9 miles, 28.04, John S. Johnson, Feb. 26, 1894.

10 miles, 31.07½, V. Bergstroem, March 27, 1919.

11 miles, 35.43 4/5, A. D. Smith, Jan. 26, 1894.

12 miles, 38.49 4/5, A. D. Smith, Jan. 26, 1894.

13 miles, 42.27 2/5, A. D. Smith, Jan. 26, 1894.

14 miles, 45.51 4/5, A. D. Smith, Jan. 26, 1894.

15 miles, 49.17 3/5, A. D. Smith, Jan. 26, 1894.

16 miles, 52.42 4/5, A. D. Smith, Jan. 26, 1894.

17 miles, 56.09 1/5, A. D. Smith, Jan. 26, 1894.

18 miles, 59.34 1/5, A. D. Smith, Jan. 26, 1894.

19 miles, 1.03.04 3/5, A. D. Smith, Jan. 26, 1894.

20 miles, 1.06.36 2/5, A. D. Smith, Jan. 26, 1894.

25 miles, 1.30.15, John Karlsen, Feb. 6, 1916.

30 miles, 1.53.20, J. F. Donohue, Jan. 26, 1893.

40 miles, 2.34.46, J. F. Donohue, Jan. 26, 1893.

50 miles, 3.15.59 2/5, J. F. Donohue, Jan. 26, 1893.

60 miles, 4.07.00 3/5, J. F. Donohue, Jan. 26, 1893.

70 miles, 4.55.00 3/5, J. F. Donohue, Jan. 26, 1893.

80 miles, 5.41.55, J. F. Donohue, Jan. 26, 1893.

90 miles, 6.25.57 3/5, J. F. Donohue, Jan. 26, 1893.

100 miles, 7.11.38 1/5, J. F. Donohue, Jan. 26, 1893.

WORLD'S RECORDS ROLLER SKATING—PROFESSIONAL

½ mile, 1.15, Ollie Moore, Chicago, 1908.

1 mile, 2.46 2/5, Rodney Peters, Feb. 11, 1909.

2 miles, 5.32, Clarence Hamilton, Aug. 10, 1909.

2 miles, 5.32, William Blackburn, 1910.

3 miles, 8.32 2/5, Clarence Hamilton, Aug. 17, 1909.

5 miles, 15.07, Ollie Moore, 1908.

10 miles, 32.41½, Harley Davidson, April 17, 1912.

15 miles, 49.15, William Blackburn, 1910.

(By Hours)

1 hour, 16 miles, E. Reynolds, 1895.

24 hours, 279 miles 319 yards, Jesse Carey, Dec. 25, 1910.

24 hours (team work), Frank Bryant and Raymond Kelly, Jan. 23, 1915, 348 miles 8 laps.

144 hours, 1,100 miles, H. Snowden, 1885.

144 hours (team race), 1,519 miles, Elsenhard and Burke, 1910.

WORLD'S MOTOR BOAT RECORDS

30 miles, 33.06, Miss America, Cowes, Eng., Aug. 10, 1920.

90 miles (three heats, each 30 miles), Miss America, Detroit, Mich., 25.37 2/5—29.35 2/5—30.80 1/5 (average 28.51), Sept. 11-13, 1920.

One mile, 46 3/10 sec. (average made at rate 77.85 miles per hour), Miss America, at Lake George, 1920.

OPEN DISPLACEMENT BOATS

"The Adieu," 38 4/10 miles per hour, defeating Canadian boat "Rainbow" at Miami, Fla., 1920. Also made record for boats of her class by doing 50 miles in 1 hour and 18 minutes, Feb. 10, 1921.

WORLD'S RECORDS—YACHTING

Most Races Sailed for America's Cup

7—Resolute won 3; Shamrock IV won 2, and two declared off, 1920.

Fastest Time Ever Made in Race

3 hours 7 min. 2 sec., Columbia (Am.), Oct. 18, 1871.

Slowest Time Ever Made in Race

10 hrs. 55 min., Aurora (English), Aug. 22, 1851.

Greatest Margin of Time of Victor (Excluding Walkovers)

39 min. 12 sec., Magic (Am.) vs. Cambria (Eng.) Aug. 8, 1870.

Smallest Margin of Time of Victor

40 sec., Vigilant (Am.) vs. Valkyrie II (Eng.), Oct. 13, 1893.

WORLD'S RECORDS IN WRESTLING

Longest Wrestling Match

8 hrs. 17 min., Geo. Bothner vs. Eugene Tunney, Montreal, Canada.

World's Record Consecutive Wins

943 bouts, Stanislaus Zybszko, started 1910 and continued till 1921. (Undefeated as yet.)

WORLD'S RECORDS IN GOLF

Making Hole in "One"

Sandy Herd, professional golfer, holds world record of having made 14 holes in "one" over Coombe course, England.

J. A. Ball, Charleston, S. C., made two holes in "one" in succession. First from 133-yd. hole, and the second from the 157-yd. mark at Newport, R. I.

Fred Poole, the one-time Yale catcher, has made two holes in "one" in one game at Boston, Mass.

Michael Brady (professional) has made two holes in "one" on the Buzzard Bay course. His first was on the fifth, and his second on the eleventh hole.

Francis X. Ouimet has one to his credit, made at Woodland in 1920.

J. H. Taylor, English professional, has a record of thirteen holes in "one" to his credit.

Only two holes in "one" have been made in championship games, one by Bob Gardner at Detroit in 1915, and the other by Deal A. Mitchell in the open championship games in 1920.

World's Record Golf Ball Drive

395 yds., James Braid, London, Eng., 1905.

WORLD'S AVIATION RECORDS

Altitude

36,020 feet, Maj. R. W. Schroeder, Dayton, O., Feb. 27, 1920.

Endurance

26 hr. 19 min. 50 sec., by Ed. Stinson (pilot) and Lloyd Bertaud (mech.), Dec. 29, 30, 1921.

24 hr. 19 min. 7 sec., Lieuts. B. Bossoutrob and Jean Bernard, Etampes, France, in Farnum Goliath, June 4, 1920.

Parachute Jump

22,000 feet, Sergt. Ensell Chambers, Feb. 22, 1921. Landed 6 miles from where he started.

Aerial Mail

2,700 miles (San Francisco to New York). Three pilots, making eight stops en route, covered distance in 25 hours 53 minutes. Average 103 miles per hour.

Speed

193 miles (per hour), Capt. De Romanet (France), on November 4, 1920.

176.9 miles (per hour), Bert Acosta (Omaha), November, 1921.

WORLD'S BALLOON RECORD

1,171 miles, Allen R. Hawley and Augustus Post, left St. Louis 4.30 P. M., October 11, 1910, and on Oct. 19 at 3.45 P. M. landed 50 miles north of Chicoutimi, Can.

WORLD'S GLIDING FLIGHT—NON-AIDED

22 min. (distance 6 miles), Rhön, Germany, Sept. 6, 1921.

WORLD'S RECORD MOUNTAIN CLIMBING

24,563 feet, Duke of The Abruzzi to the summit of "Bride Peak," near Mt. Everest.

WORLD'S RECORD—SCULLING; ROWING

1880—E. Hanlan beat E. Trickett, Nov. 15. Time, 26m. 12s.

1881—E. Hanlan beat E. C. Laycock, Feb. 14. Time, 25m. 41s.

1882—E. Hanlan beat R. W. Boyd, April 3. Time, 21m. 25s.

1882—E. Hanlan beat E. Trickett, May 1. Time, 28m.

1884—E. Hanlan beat E. C. Laycock, May 22. Time not taken.

1884—W. Beach beat E. Hanlan, Aug. 16. Time not taken.

1885—W. Beach beat T. Clifford, Feb. 28. Time, 26m.

1885—W. Beach beat E. Hanlan, March 28, Time, 22m. 51s.

1885—W. Beach beat N. Matterson, Dec. 18. Time, 24m. 11s.

1886—W. Beach beat J. Gaudaur, Sept. 18. Time, 22m. 29s.

1886—W. Beach beat Wallace Ross, Sept. 25. Time, 23m. 5s.

1887—W. Beach beat E. Hanlan, Nov. 26. Time, 19m. 55s.

1888—P. Kemp beat T. Clifford, Feb. 11. Time, 23m. 47s.

1888—P. Kemp beat E. Hanlan, May 5. Time, 21m. 36s.

1888—P. Kemp beat E. Hanlan, Sept. 28. Time, 21m. 25s.

1888—H. E. Searle beat P. Kemp, Oct. 27. Time, 22m. 44s.

1889—H. E. Searle beat W. O'Connor, Sept. 9. Time, 22m. 42s.

1890—J. Stanbury beat W. O'Connor, June 30. Time, 22m. 59s.

1891—J. Stanbury beat J. McLean, April 28. Time not taken.

1892—J. Stanbury beat T. Sullivan, May 2. Time, 17m. 26½s.

1896—J. Stanbury beat C. R. Harding, July 13. Time, 21m. 51s.

1896—J. Gaudaur beat J. Stanbury, Sept. 7. Time, 23m. 1s.

1901—G. Towns beat Jake Gaudaur. Time, 20m. 30s.

1904—G. Towns beat R. Tressider. Time, 21m. 49s.

1905—J. Stanbury beat G. Towns, July 22. Time (unofficial), 19m. 50s.

1906—G. Towns beat J. Stanbury, July 28. Time, 19m. 53 1/5s.

1907—*G. Towns beat E. Durnan, March 2. Time, 22m. 27s.

*Resigned, challenged by brother, C. Towns.

1907—W. Webb beat C. Towns, Aug. 3. Time, 20m. 45s.

1908—W. Webb beat R. Tressider, Feb. 25. Time, 20m. 28s.

1908—R. Arnst beat W. Webb, Dec. 15. Time, 19m. 52s.

1909—R. Arnst beat W. Webb, June 22. Time, 18m. 15s.

1910—R. Arnst beat G. Whelch, April 4. Time not given.

1910—R. Arnst beat E. Barry, Aug. 18. Time, 20m. 14 3/5s.

1911—R. Arnst beat Harry Pearce, July 29. Time, 19m. 46s.

1912—E. Barry beat R. Arnst, July 29. Time, 23m. 8s.

1912—E. Barry beat E. Durnan, Oct. 14. Time, 22m. 31s.

1919—A. Felton beat E. Barry, Oct. 27. Time, 25m. 40s.

1920—E. Barry beat A. Felton, Aug. 28. Time, 24m. 32s.

WORLD'S TRAP SHOOTING RECORDS
100 (or more) targets

Frank M. Broeh, of Vancouver, Wash., established record of having broken 100 or more targets 16 times.

Longest Run One Day

375—Straight. Homer Clark (professional), Chillicothe, O., June 6, 1918.

Longest Run at Two-day Tournament

400—Straight. J. R. Graham (amateur), Chicago, Ill., Aug. 31-Sept. 1, 1910.

Longest Run Four-day Tournament

422—Straight. Mark Arie (amateur), Monticello, Ill., July 22; Gilman, Ill., July 31; Bloomington, Ill., August; Chicago, Ill., Aug. 10, 1919.

591—Straight. Fred Gilbert (professional), Cherokee, Iowa, July 29; Pocahontas, Iowa, July 30; Spirit, Iowa, Aug. 4 and 5, and Hampton, Iowa, Aug. 7, 1919.

300 Targets

300—Fred Gilbert (professional), Spirit Lake, Iowa, Aug. 4 and 5, 1919.

400 Targets

397—Frank S. Wright (amateur), St. Thomas, Ont., June 2-3-4, 1919.

450 Targets

448—Rush Razee (professional), Sheridan, Wyo., June 14-15-16, 1919.

475 Targets

470—Sam A. Huntley (amateur), Boise, Ida., 1914.

500 Targets

494—Frank S. Wright (amateur), Maplewood, N. H., July 1-2-3-4, 1919.

499—Lester S. German (professional), Atlantic City, N. J., Sept. 16-17-18, 1915.

510 Targets

506—O. N. Ford (amateur), St. Louis, Mo. June 11-12-13, 1909.

525 Targets

521—Sam A. Huntley (amateur), Salt Lake, Utah, May, 1914.

560 Targets

540—Fred Gilbert (professional), Burlington, Iowa, May 17-18-19, 1909.

625 Targets

619—Homer Clark (professional), Butler, Pa., June 17-18-19-20, 1919.

World's Trap Shooting Records

John D. Adkins (U. S. Marines) at 1,000 yards made 71 hits in 71 shots, October, 1921.

John R. Bonner (N. Y. A. C.) on Feb. 5, 1921, at Mad. Sq. Garden, broke 166 clay pigeons. This is the world's indoor record.

Double Targets

96x100—William Ridley (amateur), Denver, Colo., Sept. 11, 1912.

96x100—C. B. Platt (amateur), Chicago, Ill. Aug. 22, 1917.

80 Singles, 10 Pairs, 100 Targets

100 straight, John W. Garrett (professional), Chicago, Ill., June 21, 1910.

Competitive Record, 18 Yards

200 straight, F. M. Troeh (amateur), Chicago Ill., Aug. 12, 1919.

200 straight, Bart Lewis (professional), Chicago, Ill., Aug. 12, 1919.

"Challenge Match," 18 Yards

100 straight, C. H. Newcomb (amateur), Philadelphia, Pa., Aug. 15, 1914, contest with Jesse E. Griffith, Philadelphia, Pa.

Club Shoot, 22 Yards

99 straight, Walter Huff (professional), Atlanta, Ga., July 2, 1917.

Against Time and for Score

200 straight, John W. Garrett (amateur), Colorado City, Colo., Dec. 25, 1902. Time, 30m. 13s.

1,000 Targets

965—Out of 1,000, John W. Garrett (amateur), at Colorado Springs, Aug. 6, 1904, in match with J. H. Rohrer, Colorado Springs, Colo., amateur (940). Time, 4h. 13m. Actual time, 2h. 5m.

961—Out of 1,000, Mrs. Ad. Topperwein (professional), San Antonio, Texas, July 18, 1898. Time, 4h. 13m. Exhibition.

929—Out of 1,000, Alex. Mermod (amateur), match with Fred Stone (901), St. Louis, Mo., Jan. 13, 1911. Each man shot in turn, using one gun, and against time. Time, 2h. 30m. Actual shooting time, 1h. 30m. 23s.

2,000 Targets

1,952—Mrs. Ad. Topperwein (professional), Montgomery, Ala., Nov. 11, 1916. Time, 5h. 20m. Actual shooting time, 3h. 15m. One gun used. Exhibition.

5,000 Glass Balls

4,844—By Capt. A. H. Bogardus, in 1875. Time, 6h. 13m. 45s.

Glass Ball Shooting Against Time

Capt. A. H. Bogardus broke 5,500 in 7h. 19m. 2s. at New York, Dec. 20, 1879.

Record Shooting for Month

2387x2425, Lester S. German, Aberdeen, Md. (professional), from May 26 to June 26, 1917.

Competitive Squad Records
(16 Yards) Five Men, 200 Targets

200, at Tuscaloosa, Ala., Sept. 19, 1917, by Col. Anthony H. J. Borden, Jos. Hightower, Hugh Poston and Walter Huff (professionals).

(16 Yards) Five Men, 500 Targets

497—At Maplewood, N. H., July 7, 1916, by A. C. King (99), R. L. Spotts (100), C. H. Newcomb (99), A. B. Richardson (99), Fred Plum (100) (amateurs).

World's Trap Shooting Records
Five Men, 1,000 Targets

986—At Thompsonville, Ill., April 20, 1910, by J. J. Bundy (192), R. C. Rains (194), Ira Gailbraith (200), C. G. Spencer (200), *Art Killam (200). (*Professional.)

Five Men, 2,000 Targets

1953x2000—At La Salle, Ill., May 23, 24, 25, 1916, by *Homer Clark, M. P. Arie, J. R. Jahn, F. A. Graper, William Hoon. (*Professional.)

Five Men, 3,000 Targets

2917—At Vernon, Cal., on June 6, 7 and 8, 1919, by L. S. Hawxhurst (professional), F. S. Mellus (amateur), F. M. Troeh (amateur), Fred Bair (amateur), and James W. Seavey (amateur).

Consecutive Tournaments
Two Tournaments—Two Days Each

794x800—By H. E. Poston (professional), Los Angeles, Cal., Sept. 30, Oct. 1 (397x400), and Ray, Ariz., Oct. 9-10, 1917 (397x400).

Five Tournaments—Two Days Each

2066x2100—J. S. Day (amateur), Midland, Tex., Aug. 8, 9 (434x450); Big Springs, Tex., Aug. 10, 11 (442x450); Cisco, Tex., Aug. 12, 13 (395x400); Gorman, Tex., Aug. 15, 16 (398x400); Walnut Springs, Tex., Aug. 17, 18, 1910 (397x400).

Five Tournaments—Two Two-Day and Three One-Day

942x950—Lester S. German (professional), between July 11 and Aug. 15, 1917.

Five Tournaments, One Day Each

823x830, Mark Arie, Champaign, Ill. (amateur), between July 7 and Aug. 10, 1919.

745x750, by J. R. Jahn, Long Grove, Iowa (professional), between May 4 and May 19, 1919.

719x730, by Lester S. German, Aberdeen, Md. (professional), between April 4 and May 1, 1917.

Three Tournaments, Two Two-Day and One One-Day

993x1,000, by James S. Day (amateur), at Cisco, Tex., Aug. 14; Gorman, Tex., Aug. 15-16;

Walnut Springs, Tex., Aug. 17-18, 1910; 200 targets daily. The breaks were 198, 198, 200, 198, 199.

One Tournament—Five Days

990x1,000, Frank S. Wright (amateur), at Maplewood, N. H., July 3 to 7, 1918.

Five Tournaments, One One-Day and Four Two-Day

894x900, by Fred Gilbert, Spirit Lake, Iowa (professional), between July 31 and Aug. 28, 1919.

Two Tournaments—One Three-Day and One Two-Day

839x850, by Rush Razee (professional), at Sheridan, Wyo., June 14, 15 and 16, 1919 (448x450); at Crow Agency, Mont., June 19 and 20, 1919 (391x400).

WORLD'S CRICKET RECORDS

Bowlers Who Have Over 2,000 Wickets

2107 wickets, J. B. King, London, Eng.
2044 wickets, F. F. Kelly, London, Eng.

Greatest Individual Score

628 runs (not out), A. F. Collins of Clark's House vs. North Town, Clifton, Eng., June, 1899.

424 runs, A. C. McLaren, Lancaster vs. Somerset, Taunton, Eng., July, 1895.

Greatest Score by Team

1739 runs, A. E. Stoddard's English vs. New So. Wales.

1094 runs, Melbourne Univ. vs. Essenden, Melbourne, 1898.

Longest Partnership

623 runs, Capt. Oakes and Pvt. Fitzgerald, Royal Munster Fusiliers vs. Army Service Corps, at Curragh, Ireland, 1895.

Greatest Batting Feat—Career

217 centuries, Dr. W. G. Grace, up to 1915.

Greatest Number of Centuries in Season

7 centuries (159, 100, 100, 121, 182, 110, 240), P. T. Higgins, Los Angeles, 1912.

Total Score for Season—Individual
U. S.

1748 runs by G. S. Patterson, Germantown C. C. 1892.

Canada

1509 runs, Rev. F. W. Terry, Toronto C. C. 1892.

Record Score Teams—Game

689 runs, G. S. Patterson Eleven vs. A. M. Wood's Eleven, at Philadelphia, 1894.

633 runs (8 wickets), Australia vs. Vancouver, Can., 1913.

Smallest Score on Record—Teams

0, America vs. Roseville, at Guttenberg, N. J., 1897.

Smallest Score—Int. Match

13 runs, West Indians vs. Australians, 1913.

6 runs, Winnipeg vs. Australians, 1913.

Bowling Feats

764 wickets, taken by F. R. Spofforth, England (1878), made on Australian tour. Spofforth in one match in Australia (1878) bowled down all ten wickets of opponents in each inning.

WORLD'S RECORDS—MISCELLANE-OUS

Throwing Baseball

381 ft. 2½ in., R. C. Campbell (No. Adams, Mass.), Oct. 8, 1887.

Batting Baseball

430 ft., "Babe" Ruth (New York City), June 14, 1921.

Throwing La Crosse Ball

497 ft. 7½ in., Barney Quinn, Ottawa, Sept. 10, 1892.

Throwing Cricket Ball

422 ft., R. Percival, Durham Sands, Eng., April 13, 1884.

Rising and Striking "Hurling" Ball

210 ft., M. Scully, New York, Sept. 7, 1906.

Kicking Football

200 ft. 8 in. (place kick), W. P. Chadwick, Exeter, Mass., Nov. 29, 1887.

189 ft. 11 in. (drop kick), P. O'Dea, Madison, Wis., May 7, 1898.

Medley Race

¼ mile each in walking, running, horseback, bicycle, rowing, swimming—15m. 42s., L. De B. Handley, Bayonne, N. J., Sept. 2, 1900.

Javelin Throw

215 ft. 9¼ in., Myrra (Finland), Olympic G., 1920.

204 ft. 5⅝ in. (held in middle), Lemming (Swed.), Sept. 29, 1912.

Swinging Indian Clubs (3 lb. 4 oz.)

144 hours (continuous), Martin Dobrilla, Australia, September, 1913.

Skipping the Rope

11,810 turns, J. M. Barnett (Australia), Feb. 5, 1913.

Rope Climbing

35 ft. up, 14 2/5 sec., Edward Lindenbaum, N. Y., April 21, 1914.

35 ft. 8 in. up (using hands and feet), 14 4/5 sec., C. E. Raynor, Aug. 27, 1902.

38 ft. up, 16 3/5 sec., Louis Weissman, New York, April 17, 1920.

Bending Forwards and Backwards

1700 "sit-ups" (floor), Geo. Weber, New York, October, 1921.

Bow and Arrow (Archery)

459 yds. 8 in., Inigo Simon (Turkish bow, buffalo horn), Le Touquet, France, June, 1913.

Fly Casting (4 oz. lead)

461 ft. 10 ins., Harold G. Lentz, Ocean City, N. J., July 31, 1920.

Ski Jumping

229 feet, Harry Hull, Revelstoke, B. C., Feb. 9, 1921.

235 feet, Henry Hansen (made this record but fell upon landing, Feb. 9, 1921).

Dog Racing

412 miles, Alex Holmson, with team Siberian wolf hounds (1910), in 71 h. 14m. 20s.

Winning Jockey—Most Winners

6 winners, Walter Miller (day—twice in 1906).

Season

388 winners, Walter Miller, 1906.

297 winners, Eugene Hildebrandt, 1904.

Most Dice Passes—Regular Game

22 ($60 to $8,000)—Jimmy Duffy, Oct. 11, 1920 (in game on West 47th St., New York).

Shorthand Writing

215 words a minute, Albert Schneider, Aug. 25, 1921.

Typewriting (Speed)

G. L. Hossfeld, 136 words in 1 min. (Underwood typewriter.)

Endurance Test

Sharper, an English saddle horse, ran 47 1/3 miles in 2h. 48m. at Zarskoseselo, Russia, 1887.

Alfred Adams stood on one leg consecutively for twelve hours at London, 1815.

World's Champion Hens

Lady Walnut Hill laid 876 eggs in 3 years. (Property University of Kentucky.)

Lady Victory laid 1,011 eggs in 4 years.

Adeline Gehrig threw basketball 88 ft. 6 in. at N. Y. Turn Verein, November, 1921.

Dan O'Leary, 81 years old, walked 22 miles against 5 young men, average age 26, and won in the time of 4 hours 55 minutes. (Indianapolis, Dec. 11, 1921.)

Ethical Culture School vs. Clark School. Former defeated latter at basketball by 162 baskets to 5. (World's record.) Dec. 9, 1921.

WORLD'S RECORD PURCHASE PRICE
Baseball Players

$137,500, Babe Ruth (1920), Boston A. L. to New York A. L.

$75,000, James O'Connell (1921), San Francisco P. C. L. to New York National.

$55,000, Carl Mays (1919), Boston A. L. to New York A. L.

$50,000, Tris Speaker (1916), Boston A. L. to Cleveland A. L.

$50,000, Grover C. Alexander (1918), Phila. N. L. to Chicago N. L.

$50,000, Eddie Collins (1915), Phila. A. L. to Chicago A. L.

$35,000, Frank Baker (1916), Phila. A. L. to New York A. L.

$35,000, Benny Kauff (1916), Brooklyn Feds. to New York N. L.

$22,500, Marty O'Toole (1912), St. Paul A. A. to Pittsburgh N. L.

Horses

$265,000—Tracery (foreign).

209,000—Prince Palatine (foreign).

189,000—Flying Fox (foreign).

157,500—Cyllene (foreign).

151,200—Diamond Jubilee (foreign).

150,000—Jardy (foreign).

150,000—Craganour (foreign) .

150,000—Ormonde (foreign).

150,000—Rocksand (American).

150,000—Inchcape (American).

115,000—Morvich (American).

100,000—Playfellow (American).

Poland China Hog

$35,000, Chief's Best (Indiana), 1921.

Pedigreed Bull

$100,000, King Pontiac Frayne, Algonquin, Ill., 1920.

Cat

$20,000, Silver Geberich, 1921.

A FEW OPINIONS

I have many books on sport. Your edition is one that can be relied upon. It is the best on the market with every item in all lines of sport recorded. Every newspaperman should have a copy on his desk. Send to my home address twenty-five copies, as this one may be missing every day.

PETE HERMAN,
Bantam Champion of the World.

Your book is great. After perusing it, I find there is not a record missing in any sport. It is absolutely the best publication I have ever seen. It ought to go very "big." Wishing you success, I am,

JOHNNY DUNDEE,
Junior Lightweight Champion of the World.

Your book is the greatest in its line. It's got every record in every sport. You ought to sell millions. Every sport-lover ought to have one. Send me another dozen.

CHARLIE ROSS,

World's Famous Trainer, Earl Caddock, Charlie White, Johnny Coulon, Pete Herman, Jack Britton, Freddie Welsh, Willie Jackson, Frank Klaus, Carl Morris, Jimmie Hanlon, Etc.

Say, it's a wonder. It will settle more disputes than a thousand sporting writers. Every one interested in sports will buy one, even if you asked Five Dollars a book instead of fifty cents.

LEW TENDLER.

9 781348 179559